101 GAY SEX
SECRETS REVEALED

101 GAY SEX
SECRETS REVEALED

Jonathan Bass

alyson books
los angeles

MANUFACTURED IN THE UNITED STATES OF AMERICA.

THIS TRADE PAPERBACK ORIGINAL IS PUBLISHED BY ALYSON PUBLICATIONS,
P.O. BOX 4371, LOS ANGELES, CA 90078-4371.
DISTRIBUTION IN THE UNITED KINGDOM BY TURNAROUND PUBLISHER SERVICES
LTD., UNIT 3 OLYMPIA TRADING ESTATE, COBURG ROAD, WOOD GREEN,
LONDON N22 6TZ ENGLAND.

FIRST EDITION: SEPTEMBER 2004

04 05 06 07 08 **a** 10 9 8 7 6 5 4 3 2 1

ISBN 1-55583-851-0

CREDITS
COVER AND INTERIOR ILLUSTRATIONS BY RANDAL GREY.
COVER DESIGN BY MATT SAMS.

For R., and for every admirer, arm-piece, beau, boyfriend, brother, Casanova, crush, daddy, devotee, dude, fag, flamer, freak, gentleman friend, guy, habitué, heartthrob, homo, inamorato, lover, papi, paramour, Romeo, slut, steady, stud, sugar, suitor, sweetie, tramp, trick, twink, valentine, wooer, and worshipper who made researching this book such fun. I could say it was difficult work, but I'd be lying.

CONTENTS

Introduction • 1

Chapter 1
Ready, Set—Check Yourself Before You Wreck Yourself • 3

Chapter 2
Masturbation: It's a Sure Thing • 29

Chapter 3
Seduction and "Foreplay" • 54

Chapter 4
Cock and Ball Tips • 72

Chapter 5
Doing the Butt—a Primer • 93

Chapter 6
Pole Positions • 113

Chapter 7
Accoutrements: Sex Toys and Accessories • 129

Chapter 8
How to Play Better With Others • 148

Chapter 9
Role-play, Fantasy, and Advanced Study • 170

Chapter 10
Romance, Passion, and Leaving a Lasting Impression • 194

INTRODUCTION

How difficult can it be, right? Insert tab A into slot B and repeat until orgasm. If that were the case, you'd hardly need this book. Gay sexual relations, like all good things in life, are significantly more complicated than that. So what secrets does this book hold? What will you learn about gay sex? Hopefully, you've picked up this book before you've dropped your pants. If not, read quickly.

This book is for any guy who loves dick—or is thinking he might want to give it a whirl. This book is for newly out men, men who are thinking of coming out, men who have been out for years, single men, partnered men, polyamorous men, and any guy who wants to add a little spice to his sexual repertoire. Inside you'll find sections that cover the mysteries of cruising, the subtle hints that body language reveals about potential dates, and the cues you can send to let men know you're available and interested. Soon you'll be flirting like a champ!

Whether you're a first-timer or you've been having sex with men for years, whether you've just been on a few dates or you're a veteran Casanova, whether you're a serial dater or you have a longtime boyfriend or partner—this book is certain to help you energize your sex play. How so? By revealing the secrets to planning a jealousy-free three-way, throwing a scandalous sex party (without ruining the furniture), the basic tools for invigorating role-play, and the secrets to starting a killer sex-toy collection. I'll explain the subtle differences between a lover and a fuck buddy, the basics of talking dirty, fail-safe rimming and masturbating techniques, hints and suggestions on being a good top and bottom, and of course, tips on how to send your partner to the moon with a fantastic blow job.

Now for the important disclaimer: I am not a doctor or a health care professional; this book is not a how-to manual for safe sex. Nevertheless, safe sex is a vital part of any sexual interaction. It's your inescapable duty as a sexually active man to know your HIV status—no matter how you identify your sexual orientation—and to practice responsible sex so as not to put yourself or your partners at risk. You should understand which sexual activities pose the risk of transmitting HIV and inform your partners of your HIV status. If you aren't aware of the methods of transmission of other sexually transmitted diseases such as gonorrhea and syphilis (the latter of which is on the rise in major metropolitan areas in the U.S. for the first time in years), do yourself the favor of learning. You can read more about HIV testing and sexually transmitted diseases at www.gayhealthchannel.com.

Read this book alone and try out some techniques on a new partner, or read it with a lover and practice on one another. Sex is a never-ending adventure as well as a constant learning process. Our bodies and our tastes change over time, so go in with an open mind and a willing body.

CHAPTER 1

Ready, Set—Check Yourself Before You Wreck Yourself

★★★

NO. 1   Attitude Is Everything

Before the clothes come off; before the sweat-drenched sucking, fucking, and pony rides begin; before you step foot in that cruisy bar or dance-with-your-shirt-off club (or Laundromat, Home Depot, AA meeting, or wherever you like to meet guys); before you even leave the house/apartment/your mama's basement—before you do any of these things, you must assess your own attitude. Why? A bad attitude is the single most noticeable thing about you. It's perceptible in the first 20 seconds of a conversation, and it's visible from across a room. It's practically *tangible*. It's more noticeable than your expensive Italian shoes or your painstakingly sand-blasted jeans. It doesn't matter if you had a manicure, pedicure, ass wax, and root planning just this morning. If your outlook stinks, if you're convinced that you're unwantable, undateable, unfuckable (or worse, that you're *too* hot or buff or smart or stylish to be approached), guys will sense it and move away from you as if you'd just farted on a crowded dance floor. Your bad attitude will linger around you like a brown cloud.

Imagine leaving the house for a bar or club but looking as if you're shrouded in gloom. Would you approach a gloomy you? Would you respond to a gloomy you who's cruising you? If you're going to be Dr. Doom, you'd better have your 10-inch cock and your platinum card hanging out of your pants while you're leaning back against the bar, or chances are you won't be approached tonight—or *any* night.

At the risk of getting a little bit pop-psych so early in the book: If your demeanor is confident but not too haughty, comfortable and relaxed but not complacent, you will appear a little taller, your smile will beam a bit brighter. With the proper confidence and a little charm, you could wear a meat hat into a vegan restaurant and no one would show you to the door. Whether we like it or not, appearances do count for something, and your attitude plays a part in your physical presence—luckily, attitude is the easiest part of your appearance to enhance.

First, primp and preen a little bit before performing a self-diagnosis. Give yourself a good look in the mirror and make a mental note to keep your posture upright and your facial expression bright—or at least not too stern. Slumped and dour just won't do. Never, under any circumstances, conduct an attitude check under fluorescent lights. They are uncannily unflattering, and they're unlikely to improve any potential attitude problems. We don't need you to go spiraling into depression when you're all gussied up to paint the town pink.

Second, determined horniness is fine—it can help you land a hottie in bed. But don't go into a potential hookup situation with a "do or die" (or perhaps a "do him or die trying") approach, because if you don't get your man, you're likely to be a little bummed out. Even the hottest of guys strikes out occasionally. It's life in the big, gay city, and "thanks but no thanks" is nothing to be depressed over. It's our lot to dig in, work that mojo, and have fun. It's all for naught if you're not having fun.

NO. 2 Dress to Impress

Who was it who said "Clothes make the man"? Whenever I hear it, it's always a retail clerk working on commission. Whether you buy into the theory or not, many gay men do, and it pays off to have a personal sense of style. But don't despair; you can develop a personal sense of style without shelling out the big bucks for haute couture. Some basic items in some stylish combinations will have all the boys asking, "See that natty dresser? Is he gay, or is he British?"

Unless you're on the cutting edge of fashion (and despite our delusions of grandeur, we can't all be) a second opinion will come in handy. A reliable second opinion can keep us from convincing ourselves that suspenders are making a comeback, or that the International Male catalog should be used for anything other than cheap porno (jerk off to it, but never actually *buy* from the catalog), or from wearing clever T-shirts with slogans like NO ONE KNOWS I'M GAY. And—God forbid—unless you're a designer, you should *never* wear your own designs.

If you aren't clothing-savvy, don't despair. That's what friends are for. A good friend or a fashion-conscious acquaintance can help you select a few appealing combinations from your wardrobe. A relatively painless shopping trip can fill in any gaps. Invite the trusted friend over on a quiet Sunday afternoon, provide a margarita or two, and dig through your closet until you have at least one cocktail party outfit and several options for a more casual environment like a bar or club. These should give you a wide variety of options that will fit the bill for most modern gay social situations.

A very basic cocktail party outfit consists of a pair of pants in black, gray, navy, or brown (flat fronts are the most flattering); a button-down shirt in any neutral color, or wine, pale blue, navy, or black (the more adventurous can pick a stripe or a print according to the season's styles); a black or brown belt to match your shoes; and black or brown shoes. Darker is usually less casual. Forget all the old fashion rules about no black with navy and no gray with brown. Just trust your second opinion.

Variations include wearing a blazer with a polo-style shirt, or a cashmere or merino wool sweater. A couple rules of thumb: Your clothing should get progressively darker from head to toe (your pants should be darker than your shirt, your socks and shoes should be darker than your pants), and pants should touch the top of your shoes. You should also make the acquaintance of a reputable dry cleaner so you know where to take the clothes after they've been yanked off you in the heat of passion and wadded up on the floor beside the bed.

Skip the shorts, jeans, sneakers, and sandals for now unless you're in L.A. or the Bahamas. Your dinner-party or cocktail-party host will be impressed. In today's more casual world, your cocktail-party outfit can be worn to the theater, a nice restaurant, the opera, or most anyplace a suit would have been worn in the past.

Your more casual clothes for a bar or club environment should include one or two pairs of well-fitting jeans, some T-shirts with a flattering fit, and casual shoes or sneakers. Don't get your friendly fashion consultant liquored up too quickly—you'll want his or her rational judgment when you try on the pants you think flatter your ass. Get an honest opinion.

Find out, if you don't already know, whether your favorite club has a no-athletic wear policy (for team logos and athletic shoes—usually a policy in straight clubs in large cities) or whether your club has an outdoor patio that gets cold at night (you'll need another layer or jacket). If you're heading from a more casual to a less casual environment, just wear a nice T-shirt under your button-down shirt and strip layers as you go.

Remember that not all jeans and T-shirts are made equal—quality counts here, both in manufacturing and cut. Pay attention to clothes that fit your body type. And damn it, ditch all your old stonewashed jeans, overalls, three-quarter-length pants, and free T-shirts from defunct dot-coms. Eliminate any clothes from your closets that you haven't worn for two years. Take them to a local charity, get a receipt for a tax write-off, and don't look back.

These are just general tips. If you've got a look that works for you, then work it, baby. If you only wear 501s and your favorite brand of white undershirt, then by all means go forth and cruise in that outfit. But you shouldn't be afraid to consider the possibility that another brand of white undershirt or a different kind of jeans might fit you a bit better.

When you're ready to go out, imagine the environment you're heading into. How will the crowd be dressed? Will you get hot and sweaty from dancing? Will you be outside? Then pick a combination that will make you feel comfortable and sexy.

NO. 3 Apply the Real Estate Mantra to Hookups: Location, Location, Location

Where you go to meet guys determines in large part the kind of guy you're likely to meet. Sounds reasonable, right? If you're at the zoo and you want to see monkeys, you go to the monkey house, not the penguin tanks. Similarly, if you like to whine that you never meet stable, relationship-oriented guys in bathhouses, or that none of the guys you meet in AA will go out for a drink with you, you won't get much sympathy here.

It stands to reason that if you're looking for other 22-year-olds, don't head for a piano bar. Go someplace 22-year-olds go. Likewise, if you're 45 and interested in meeting guys your own age, don't get a ticket to the upcoming circuit party.

Granted, unlikely as it sounds, sometimes charming, successful, 30-somethings venture into a twinkfest at the 18-and-over dance club. But if you're *looking* for a charming, successful 30-something, then demographically speaking, he's going to be outnumbered, and finding him will be like finding a small, sharp sewing implement in a big pile of grass-like livestock feed.

I like to say *"La variedad es la especia de la vida."* ("Variety is the spice of life"—clichés sound better in another language.) Still, it makes good sense to know what you're in for when you head out on a manhunt. In larger cities you can find any and all of the cruising locales listed below. In smaller towns you may be more limited in your options and a wider variety of types will congregate at any given milieu. A little cruising primer:

Neighborhood bars are good for a quick drink, but aren't ideal for finding casual hook ups. They are called neighborhood bars because the fags from the neighborhood hang out there. Let's say you meet a cute local, sweet-talk him up to his apartment, then never call again. Before you can say beer bust, he'll have told his friends, the bartender, and anyone sitting at the stool next to him how you did him wrong. You won't be able to set foot in the bar again.

My friend Robert, 27, used to drag a gang of us out to his favorite neighborhood gay bar in L.A. for the cheap beer, the pinball machines, and the tacky five-year-old pop music playing on the jukebox. We danced and drank and were a good 20 years younger than anyone else in the place; we were simultaneously the objects of lust and

suspicion. As soon as we were sufficiently liquored up, we moved on to a place more suitable for meeting guys born in our own geologic era.

Hustler bars are good for picking up a hustler (natch).

Since they don't post signs outside that say "This is a place where older guys pick up younger guys and pay them to have sex/clean the bathrooms in the nude/dress them up in baby clothes," you'll have to rely on word of mouth to identify the hooker hangouts. Unless you're experienced in that department, move on down the road for now.

When I was in my early 20s, my friend Jon took me to a rather notorious hustler bar a few times, though on my first visit I didn't know that it was notorious, nor that it was a hustler bar. Because we were significantly younger than the nonhustler clientele, each time we went in, someone offered to buy us a drink or two—perhaps mistaking us for rent boys (it was strangely flattering). When we didn't reciprocate by climbing onto the laps of the generous gentlemen and whispering sweet (or nasty) nothings into their ears, we were dismissed quickly by the older men and soon felt rather unwelcome. It was good for a free drink but also a few dirty looks. These places mean business, so try the free drink thing, but only if you're under 25 and you get your first drink and go.

The **see-and-be-seen bar** is the kind of establishment that pops up frequently in gay ghettos. They're often renovated sweatshops or slaughterhouses, featuring exposed brick and internally lit urinals, and they appear and disappear quickly—depending as they do on the fickle whims of the tragically trendy. The patrons are usually joyless pretty people who are 20- or 30-something and immaculately attired. This kind of venue is full of pecs and Prada, and it's hard for guys to meet other guys there because, while conversation can still occasionally flourish, most of these pretty boys are constantly on the lookout—often over your shoulder—for someone prettier than you.

Dance clubs are places where the music determines the makeup of the crowd. Alternative rock nights bring out a parade of piercings and tattoos (and are primarily responsible for the resurgence of the mullet among nonlesbians). Pop club nights bring out a young 20s crowd who like mouthing the words to the latest Madonna remix. DJ dance nights and after-hours clubs attract rave kids and crowds of buff 20-somethings who sport a water bottle stuffed into one back pocket and a T-shirt stuffed into the other. It's a pretty scene, but the guys are very often chemically enhanced.

Art museums and galleries bring out all sorts, from sensitive, young artist types with sketchpads in hand, to wealthy, more mature art lovers. Camp out near the Greek and Roman statuary and you're sure to find a homo or two admiring the tree trunk-like quads on a Hercules or a Zeus. **Benefit galas and fund-raisers** attract an urbane, financially secure, socially aware crowd, often 40 and up. Younger men are found here less often. **Gay film festivals** bring out an age-diverse crowd of gay filmmakers, young gay film students, and older film patrons. If you meet a prospective playmate here, just be sure to have at least one favorite gay film in mind, so when you're asked you can respond confidently. **Gay sports clubs** for activities such as softball, soccer, or rugby can be found in most cities, and the benefits are obvious: getting a little exercise with a bunch of buff gay men.

But also remember this: Anywhere you go, there are likely other gay men going there too, so keep your gaydar on.

NO. 4

Be Acquainted With Bar Etiquette and Have a Plan of Attack

Now that we've examined some of the various places where gay men might meet one another, we'll explore the quintessential gay natural environment: the gay bar. It's a habitat native to the homo, and it comprises its own special rituals and taboos that require close examination. There are definitely other places to meet men these days, but it still makes sense to know your way around in this setting.

Pacing, positioning, and endurance are key here. In any bar, it's good to have a plan of attack—an approach that will maximize your potential for meeting guys and a battle posture that will make you look confident and desirable. In other words, you need to master some techniques that will enhance your Cruising Credibility Factor (CCF). Just like that white-haired old man on *Mutual of Omaha's Wild Kingdom,* you want to sit back in the studio and make your khaki-suited field lackey do all the armadillo-catching work. Too much effort diminishes your CCF. You want to be in the right place at the right time so you can meet the guys you're interested in (or so they can meet *you*).

The first issue at hand is when to arrive. If you frequent a particular set of homo haunts, you should make a mental note of the time the bars open and close, the hours when they start to get busy, and when, if ever, long lines start to appear outside—making allowances for holidays, gay pride festivals, and in the case of my hometown, religious conventions (the gay bars were always packed!).

Once inside, survey the territory by taking a walk around the place. Now is your chance to do some hi-byes—don't linger too long chatting with casual acquaintances, but take note of whether they have new, charming friends in their company. During your hi-byes, make a note of where in the bar the cute boys are. You'll want to return to those places. If you're properly placed and project a self-assured exterior, the guys will come to you.

My friend Gus has several bar rules that he and his friends dutifully employ in any gay social environment. These rules—useful once you're in the prime people-watching spot—are designed to enhance CCF and have always worked for him. Gus, who is cute but 5 foot 7 when he stands on a phone book, ends up going home with tall, gorgeous hunks with alarming frequency. Below is Gus's strategy to draw these men to him:

★ Don't chew gum, ice, or your cocktail stirrer. At best it makes you look immature or neurotic. At worst, you look like a classless subway tart. And by the way, that stirrer is not a straw.

★ Don't sit—ever! Besides messing up the drape of a nice shirt, sitting can make you look lazy or aloof and uninterested in the bar's sexual potential.

★ Always appear to be having fun. You'll instantly look more desirable. (Gus knew about the attitude check—see Secret #1).

To Gus's rules, I add my own:

★ Stay out of dark corners. No one will venture into a dark corner just to see who is there. You need to be visible.

★ Don't stand under direct overhead lighting. (You'll look like a jack-o'-lantern.)

★ Don't order a froufrou cocktail, or anything blue, or any drink that comes with an umbrella; those drinks are for sorority girls. Men order a cocktail or a beer. Exceptions include the bar's specialty drinks, if they have cool names like "the scorpion" and *any* drink you order in a tiki lounge. If it takes more than 30 seconds to make, tip the bartender well and order something easier next time.

★ If you arrive with friends, make sure you spend enough time apart from them that it's clear to other guys that you're single and available. You can do this with a solo trip to the bar or a walk around the joint.

So you've given the bar the once-over and you've had a cocktail, when suddenly from your flatteringly lit vantage point, where you are standing confidently (but not chewing gum) and perhaps holding a whiskey and Coke or a bottled beer (but not a blue Hawaiian), you see a cute stranger in a cool vintage jacket walk up to the bar. He's definitely a guy you'd like to talk to...over breakfast. You want to buy him a drink, but if you're a novice, there's a bit of drink-buying etiquette to consider.

If you can get to the bar first, let the bartender know you'd like to buy a drink for the cute guy. Be specific in describing which guy, and it's okay if the cutie overhears you flattering him: "I'd like to buy a drink for that handsome guy in the blue jacket—the one with the beautiful eyes." When the drink arrives and the bartender tells him who bought it, he may come over to say hi. But don't expect him to come over. If he doesn't, then *you* go over and say hi. Any decent guy will say thanks and allow you to introduce yourself. (For more on chatting him up, see Secret #7.)

If you are closer to the guy than the bar, say hi and ask

Mr. Dreamy Eyes what he's drinking, then order it for him, along with one for yourself (looks a little more casual and not as though you were waiting for him, even if you were). Alternatively, if the cute guy is sitting near the bar but isn't ready to order, tell the bartender you'll buy the guy his next drink, then go over and say hi. For all of these scenarios, you'll need the ear and the aide of the bartender, so it pays to tip your bartender well on your own first order.

Voilá! You're talking with the cute guy. If he's partnered or not interested, that's okay. Just roll with the punches, tell him it was nice meeting him, and move on. You're not obligated to spend too much time with anyone, especially if he's not a prospective date.

NO. 5 Dodging Zombies

It's nice to imagine that there's a patron saint or deity out there, who watches our bar behavior and balances the dating scales of us mere horny mortals. This deity—let's imagine he's a modern-day Dionysus, the Greek god of wine—would make careful note of the times we buy a drink for a prospective date in our lusty pursuit of a roll in the hay, and Dionysus would make sure that in due time someone would buy us that drink and attempt to seduce us in return. Call it cocktail karma (emphasis on *cock*).

Well, if he does exist, that Dionysus is a sneaky bastard. Just when you're looking the other way, he sends you an extra from *The Night of the Living Dead*, who's determined to buy you a drink and follow it up with some foul-breathed conversation. This bar zombie—be he old or young, messily drunk or heinously ugly—is someone you wouldn't be caught dead with in the bright light of day. Not only do you not ever want to imagine fooling around with this "Thriller" video reject, you don't want him messing up your precious CCF by appearing to be his date.

It's best not to be trapped by these zombies, so keep yourself out of narrow corners. But if you do get cornered and he offers you a drink, be gracious and then, without wasting too much time, move on. Don't say you'll be back. A polite thanks is sufficient. *Always* be polite, and not just 'cause your mama said so. Gay communities, even ones in large cities, can be gossipy and insular. The zombie you dodge (tactfully) today may be the client or business associate you work with in a few months. Plus, there's that karma thing.

NO. 6 Use a Friend's Sober (or More Sober) Judgment

If birds of a feather can do it, then so can homos—flock together, that is. Having a friend around with whom you're not sexually involved is psychologically important, whether you're in a romantic relationship, casually dating, or just bed-hopping. Having a gay friend around means that you have a person to tell all your stories about the previous night's sexual encounters after you hooked up with a superstud on the dance floor. That friend is someone with whom you'll commiserate once you've been spurned after a pickup attempt, and he will scrape your ass off the dance floor if—next time—you get too wasted to go home with the superstud. This friend can also steer you away from the hookup you'd regret in the morning.

My young friend Jason never takes my advice on anything—except when we're out at a bar or club and he's had a cocktail or two (or five). God forbid he should take my advice about his wildly unorthodox facial hair or his insistence on saying "bro." The only time he ever takes my advice is when he has wandered off and returned some time later with a potential hookup.

Jason knows that my beer blindness doesn't kick in until at least a couple of cocktails after his has, so by default I'm a better zombie judge. If the guy he brings back is missing some teeth and he's obviously not a hockey player, or if I've already seen the guy blowing someone in the corner of the bathroom, I'll say something subtle like, "Nice to meet you, (fill in the blank). Jason, I just heard them say that your car is being towed." Jason gets the hint and has an immediate excuse to move away from the guy, at which point I can enumerate my objections in private. The following day, Jason usually remembers just enough to be grateful for the cock block.

A good friend is someone who will also realize the importance of a good hookup and won't whine or pout about being left behind if you get the opportunity to score. While it's polite to contact the person you arrived at the bar or club with to let him know that you want to leave with someone else, it's vital to make sure you each have a way home. If your friend drove, then he's cool, so long as he's not drunk and planning to drive. If you drove, give your friend enough cash to take a taxi home. It's only polite, especially since you're the one leaving him. If he's the one hooking up and leaving you, be sure you have cab fare for yourself.

There are some potential dangers in the gay buddy system: While heteros usually have same-gender platonic friends and opposite-gender sex partners, gay men tend to have male friends and male sex partners. Therein lies the potential to confuse a friendly relationship with a romantic or a sexual one, especially after a night of carousing and drinking. Some guys I know have generated a group of friends from guys they've dated or slept with and decided early on that romance wasn't in their future. For simplicity's sake, it's best to keep friends and hookups as separate as possible.

NO. 7 Getting From the Bar to Your Place (or His)

So you're in the bar and you've made small talk with a few cuties, yet no one has offered to take you to his house to show you his collection of etchings. Nor have you felt the itch to mention your collection of Victorian dildos. You might wonder: Was the moment not right? Was my body language betraying me? Did I say something too corny too soon?

Making the moves on a hot guy—or responding to the moves of the gorgeous man who just bought you a drink—can be incredibly varied, but there are some universal techniques that will help you move from point A (bar) to point B (bed).

The first technique is body language. Like your attitude

(Secret #1), your body language is a nonverbal way to express your sexual availability and your interest in someone. Knowing a bit about body language can also help you decipher signals from the guys you meet. Your attitude is in good shape, and it should be reflected in your posture: shoulders back, tummy in, head up. Don't cross your arms (it's a defensive posture) and keep your hands out of your pockets (an insecure posture). Instead, when the hot guy comes up to you, maintain eye contact as long as he does. It's a not so subtle sign of attraction, albeit usually a subconscious one.

Second, make your first words count by saying something honestly flattering, instead of giving a pickup line, no matter how clever or well-rehearsed. If you like his shoes, say so. If you like his smile, tell him so. The point here is that the more honest you are with a tidbit of flattery, the less likely you are to have to follow up your opening line with a string of lies. Telling him you're on leave from NASA astronaut training, though impressive, is bound to require a few back-up lies.

Back to body language: When he starts to tell you where he got his shoes, or that he needed braces in the fifth grade, look him in the eye (or look at his mouth, another subconsciously arousing gesture) and listen. Treat everything he says as if it's the most fascinating insight you've heard all day.

Keep your nervous fidgeting to a minimum, even if you're nervous. A slow, measured rate of speech, and slightly slower, very deliberate actions are cooler, more seductive. By slowing things down a bit and not resorting to nervous activities, you'll project an aura of being calm and collected. The vibe you project will be that you are incredibly comfortable with yourself, and that he should be comfortable with you too.

Learn to read his signals too. When his pupils dilate and blinking increases, or if he angles his body toward you, those are unconscious signs of attraction. If you blink somewhat more frequently, he may subconsciously pick up on your signal too.

A third technique is to keep up the momentum by not giving him a chance to get bored, as if you're deciding what to do next. If you're in close quarters in a bar, touch his arm occasionally when you're talking to him. If the place is noisy, lean over and tell him something close in his ear. This is also a good opportunity for lightly touching his thigh or ass.

Fourth, and perhaps most important, be up-front. If you've got the hots for the guy and are interested in taking him home, you could certainly say so. It's almost certain that you'd get an immediate response. Whatever you do, don't be coy. A bar, especially a gay bar, is a place where hookups are the norm, so you don't have to pretend that you're in the place just for the beer and the music.

What to say? Well, funny as it is, "Got any Irish in you?" probably won't seal the deal. If you are going to use a line like "Come here often?" then make sure the irony is clear. If he laughs, you're on your way. No cheesy lines rehearsed? Ask him where he's going afterward and whether he'd like to join you.

NO. 8

Know the Difference Between Fuck Buddies and Lovers

The concept is simple: Your fuck buddy is anyone with whom you occasionally or regularly have hot, nasty, mind-blowing, wall-climbing, acrobatic sex—minus the emotional attachment. Your fuck buddy can be a good friend with whom you just have sex (not a great idea, frankly). Or he can be an acquaintance whom you know just well enough to know that you want his body and he wants yours—and there are absolutely no plans for joint checking accounts, weddings in Massachusetts, or shopping at the Pottery Barn together.

It's not strictly a gay phenomenon, but it's a concept that seems really well-suited to us faygelehs. The old cliché is that women show emotion and intimacy by making love, and guys just like to have sex—no deep emotional connection required. If true, then gay men have the fuck buddy racket sewed up. Guys can have sex without emotional attachments, and since gay men like to have sex with other men—hey, there seems to be no downside, right?

There are definitely benefits to having a fuck buddy. First, the sex is purely recreational and can be a great sexual outlet for guys whose work or personal lives don't allow a lot of opportunity for dating or meeting single guys. Second, for closeted men, this is a sexual relationship that can exist entirely within the privacy of your bedroom or the local motel. You won't be dragged to your fuck buddy's cousin's wedding and have to fumble over lame euphemisms like "roommate" or "coworker" when meeting the meringued bridesmaids. You may never even have to meet anyone in his sphere of friends and family. Be warned, though: The fuck buddy system can be a deterrent to coming out. If closeted guys can suck dick and fuck in private, they may delay coming out. A third benefit of having a fuck buddy is that it's much safer than cruising for anonymous sex in parks, public toilets, malls, university library bathrooms, alleyways, and the like.

If you've got a fuck buddy or are considering getting one, the system has some unwritten rules that will help avoid confusing having a sex partner with romance.

★ Make it clear to your fuck buddy that your meetings aren't romantic dates; they're sex dates. In other words, it's not actually dating at all.

★ Limit the duration of your encounters to the time it takes to get off as many times as you two like. Don't linger too long afterward for conversation or cuddling.

★ If you start to have feelings for your fuck buddy, let him know as soon as possible. Some long-term relationships do actually start out this way, so maybe he feels the same way you do. But if he's not on the same page, or even reading the same book, be prepared to cut off the relationship totally. There are few things worse than having sex with someone you really care for, while knowing he's not romantically interested.

Here's the bottom line: Keep romance and sex separate in this arrangement. Obviously, this relationship isn't for everyone, and it usually doesn't last indefinitely, but a little communication and laying down some common understanding can help you avoid complicating your no-strings arrangement.

No. 9

Labels—They Ain't Just for Designer Jeans Anymore

The labels we're talking about here are the ones we use to define ourselves as sexual beings. Though we should resist the urge to be totally defined by simple labels, they do serve an important function and merit some special consideration.

At the most basic level they describe our gender identity (male, female, transgender, intersex, and variations on gender like butch and fem/femme); our sexual orientation (gay, lesbian, bisexual, straight, queer, curious); our races (black, white, Latino, Asian, Native American, mixed); and a whole host of other physical attributes, too many to list. Anyone who has read the Men Seeking Men personals in a newspaper has seen this daunting use of labeling acronyms: "GWM in2 BDSM ISO HIV-Str8/Bi LM, 8+."

As gay men, we tend to use different labels to define ourselves within the larger gay community: bears, twinks, daddies, drag queen, straight-acting, blue collar, swimmers build, gym rat, chub, submissive, etc. The labels most often used in the bedroom are top, bottom, and versatile, along with variations like bossy bottom and dominant top. The trick with labels is to make judicious use of them but not to be ruled by them.

It's important to remember that our definitions of ourselves can vary. Ron, 30, a friend from my hometown always considered himself a top, but he says that changed when he met Tim, 32.

"I met Tim at a show where my friend's band was playing. He was so cute that I just marched up to him and asked him his name. He wasn't shy, so we started flirting right away—he said I had great eyes, which made my knees weak. He was driving his friends a long distance home that night, so we couldn't go home together. Instead we exchanged e-mail addresses and continued our flirting over e-mail.

"He told me he was 95% top, and I told him I was mostly a top too. We'd both bottomed before but preferred fucking. I was disappointed that I probably wouldn't get to fuck him—he had the cutest round, firm ass. But we made a dinner date, then had some drinks and came back to my apartment. As soon as I pulled his cock out of his pants, something went off in my head, and I knew I wanted him to fuck me. He did, and it wasn't easy, but I loved it. The next time we met, he fucked me again, and it was a little easier, and I loved it then too.

"Long story short, we've been dating for a year, and I don't think of myself as a top anymore. Sometimes we switch since I still like being on top occasionally, but I wouldn't trade roles permanently for anything. I love the way he fucks me."

The moral of Ron's story is that you must be prepared to change your labels when the old ones don't fit you anymore.

The same labels that we use to define ourselves sexually can be the ones that keep us in a sexual rut, since gay men often see their "types" in terms of labels. Guys who identify too closely with their self-imposed labels often get caught up in dating other men who are their virtual clones. In personals jargon, it often looks like this: "White athletic male, 25, seeks same"; or "Latin male,

33, seeks other hung men—no Asians, no fats, no fems."

There's nothing wrong with having preferences—the loins want what they want. But closing yourself off to nature's booty bounty is shortsighted at best and can be bigoted in its worst incarnations. Just because you like tall, dark men doesn't mean a short redhead might not one day get your little general to stand and salute—don't deny it just because you didn't expect it. If you're used to dating only white guys, that doesn't mean a beautiful black or Asian man won't float your boat. *Vive la différence*—and for a few reasons, not the least of which is that we wouldn't want to be accused of the discrimination we so hate when it comes from homophobes.

The best reason to embrace our diversity, however, is that it takes a whole lot of varied experiences to make a well-rounded person. Just because you've been eating white bread your whole life, don't pass up the chance to have that sandwich on Jewish rye. You may love it.

NO. 10 Being Out and Proud

Let's start off this section by saying that most of us have been closeted at one point in our lives, whether during childhood or adolescence or into adulthood; some remain closeted into middle age and beyond. Coming out is a very personal journey and is more or less difficult depending on your own feelings about being gay or bisexual, your family and community environment, and other personal factors.

The how-to of coming out is the matter for hundreds of

other books, so you'll have to look elsewhere for that kind of advice. My duty here is to say that being out is beneficial to your mental health, your sex life, and the gay community at large.

Being closeted is to lead your life in secrecy, keeping your sexuality and romantic relationships separate from your family, work, and friendships. Even if a man is openly gay with his friends but not his work colleagues or family, he must quarantine off a portion of his person and constantly keep secrets, which usually result in feelings of shame and claustrophobia.

There are some fundamental benefits to being out when it comes to sex and relationships. Embracing your complete sexuality is incredibly liberating. Taking charge of your sexuality by fully embracing it can be an experience that spills over into other aspects of your life. The more honest you are with yourself and your loved ones, the more confident and relaxed you'll be.

There are drawbacks to being closeted and to being involved with a closeted man. Men who remain closeted are men who must keep secrets from some people in their lives, and therefore aren't fully emotionally available. In many cases, not being out prevents men from meeting other guys, from having a fulfilling sex life, and from forming lasting relationships. Closeted men often won't go socialize in publicly gay environments like bars or dance clubs, often choosing instead to put themselves at risk with anonymous hookups from blind online booty calls or from cruising parks or tearooms. I've known gay men who refuse to go to gay-themed movies at the local multiplex for fear of being outed. Their chances of meeting men are diminished substantially.

Being openly gay is a benefit to the gay community at

large as well. The more people who know an openly gay person, the more people will be sympathetic to gay equal rights. The environment will be more conducive to more gay people coming out, and the effect will be cumulative.

Okay, enough rah-rah! Just get out there, come out already, and encourage and support your friends who need help coming out of the closet.

CHAPTER 2

Masturbation: It's a Sure Thing

★★

NO. 11

The Art of Sex for One

Masturbation is the first order of business in gay sexual experiences. Since I'm a man, I'm working with the same equipment you are. Consequently, it makes sense that the better I am at a little self-love, the better I'll handle *your* trouser snake. Likewise, I'll be better at letting you know how I like my munchkin punched. (How many goofy penis/masturbation euphemisms do you think I can use in two sections? Go on and count them in Secrets #11 and #12. We're up to three so far.)

Luckily, masturbation comes naturally to most guys—and with good reason: Every time we get dressed and undressed, we see our genitals and we're reminded of sex. Every time you feel a stirring in your loins, the impulse to shake your sugar tree comes without much thought—it's natural. We shouldn't deny the impulse to romance our own bones. We just have to make sure we don't do it on the subway or in a crowded hotel lobby. Publicly badgering your witness will get you thrown into jail.

By the time adolescents discover the joys of yanking their doodles, their parents, teachers, religious authority figures, and other kids have usually conspired to fill their heads with outdated Victorian attitudes that make masturbation seem irresponsible and dirty. Who came up with the idea that bangin' your bacon would make you go blind? Preposterous! Who decided that the devil's handshake is only for guys who aren't having sex? Poppycock! Who said a little closet Frisbee will grow hair on your palms? Have you *ever* seen anyone with hair on his palms?

These old-school ideas spring from the fact that—until the test tube baby—heterosexual sex was the only human method for reproduction. It was decided somewhere along the line that reproduction was sex's *only* real function. As evolved beings who needn't merely survive on this planet, we can recognize sex as the act of giving pleasure to someone you love, as a social activity, and as pure fun. Yet the residue of guilt hangs over many of us, causing some folks to consider masturbation the last resort of the horny and bored, or for those who can't get a date with a live person. Foolishness! While a good wank isn't a bad idea if you're feeling bored, lonely, or horny, it's emphatically not an act of desperation.

There's nothing wrong with masturbating. In fact,

there's plenty that's great about it (take a look at Secret #12). Most men masturbate, and why not? As Woody Allen said, "It's sex with someone you love." Truman Capote said, "The good thing about masturbation is that you don't have to dress up for it." You can jack your beanstalk with a lover, a hookup, a friend, or a baseball team. You can do it in your bed, on the couch, on the floor, in the bathtub, in the shower, in the steam room at the gym (as my friend Doug likes to do—he also likes getting "caught"). You can do it on a train, on a plane (be kind to your traveling companions and bait your hook in the lavatories), in the bathroom at your office building, or anywhere the mood strikes, assuming you have a little bit of privacy or a like-minded crowd.

Are there any real dangers to your psyche from masturbating? It's far more likely that totally abstaining from masturbation will have negative psychosexual effects. As for physical dangers, there is no evidence that masturbation has any affect whatsoever on the growth or shape of your penis or your semen production. So how do you know if you're assaulting your friendly weapon a little too much? Well, if it's keeping you from wanting sex with a partner, if it's holding you back from leaving the house to meet eligible men, if your fat Albert is turning blistery and purple from your five-finger torture, well, then you might think about giving it a rest. (Since your cock is made of tissues and skin, it's prone to chafing if it gets too much friction.) Otherwise, enjoy the orgasm machine nature gave you.

NO. 12

Get Jizzy With It
(It's Good for You!)

Beginning several hundred years ago, there were charlatans who claimed that counting with your 21st digit would cause insanity and physical ailments. They also offered a remedy—the useless snake oil they were selling. But that's when it was pretty easy to invent a bogus ailment and sell a cure. Modern medical science has finally caught up with us masturbators, extolling the wank as a harmless sex-positive activity. Even former Surgeon General Joycelyn Elders got on the bandwagon and gave the okay to stroking the baloney pony. (But she got fired for it, so let's give J.E. a little shout-out, shall we?) Despite all the benefits and the endorsement of the country's top medical official, masturbation's bad reputation has stuck, just like the sticky, well-used pages of an Abercrombie & Fitch catalog.

How can something so right feel so right? Trust your instincts and your groin on this one—there are many physical and psychological advantages to taking little Elvis to Graceland. In an effort to create a more jerk off-friendly world, here are just a few of the reasons you *should* do the five-knuckle shuffle:

★ Jacking off helps create positive associations with sex and helps maintain a sex-positive philosophy. Sex is good!
★ The art of manhandling your man handle is handy to know—you won't always have a partner within reach when you need sexual healing.
★ A little Southern comfort can spark up your libido.

★ Erections are like exercise for your dick: Use it so you don't lose it.

★ A big date with Rosy Palms can teach you about stimulating yourself. This comes in handy when you're in bed with a new fella, and he wants to know how to touch, stroke, and rub you all the way to the moon.

★ Do-it-yourself sex can teach you to control your own sexual response. Through your one-handed workouts, you can learn to identify the sensations that signal your preorgasmic stages of arousal—the moment just before you pop your cork. When you can recognize that moment, you can take steps to prolong sex (Secret #49) and keep yourself from crossing the finish line if your partner is just leaving the starting gate.

★ When you're making like Han Solo and stroking your wookie, you can have sex for one as often as you like, with as many appliances or toys as you like, with food, special clothes, mirrors, or anything that turns you on—even stuff that might freak out a partner.

★ Loading your torpedo bay releases mood-elevating endorphins that help ward off depression. It can perk you up after a crappy day.

★ Polishing your china is a great way to help you get to sleep (right after you clean up).

★ Using the force on your meat saber is a much better boredom solution than smoking or overeating.

★ Following your bliss is a good way to satisfy yourself sexually when a partner isn't willing or able to get you off, or when you want sex more than he does.

★ Coming to grips with yourself is free. You don't have to buy your own cock dinner and drinks before you get naked with it.

★ Regular ejaculation flushes out the prostate gland, which can prevent infections. Recent medical evidence suggests that working a cramp out of your love muscle on a regular basis (on the average of five times a week between age 20 and 50) is good preventive care to help ward off prostate cancer later in life.

★ Solo knob-rubbing, where you don't have any sexual contact with another person, is a totally safe sexual activity and does not put you at risk of contracting HIV or other STDs.

★ Pocket pool burns calories—I'm not sure how many, but it's got to be more than you'd burn watching game shows.

So what are you waiting for? Unzip your pants, pull out that Pennis the Menace, and get cracking that fat! By the way, there were 43 penis or masturbating euphemisms in the last two secrets.

NO. 13 Know Thyself, Know Thy Penis

The best way to make sure you know what's going on downstairs is to learn a little anatomy lesson. Your penis is just loaded with lovely little nerve endings, and it makes sense to know where they are. (Don't worry, there's no quiz.) Just think of it as playing doctor. Go get a friend, get naked, and point out the interesting bits on each other as you read this chapter.

It's been called a boner, the bone pony, the meat 'n' bones, your man muscle, your muscle of love, Russell the love muscle, or the xylobone (okay, nobody really calls it the xylobone, but go ahead and start calling it that if you like—just make sure you tell 'em you read it here first). In fact, there aren't actually any bones or muscles in your boner. So what is it? Let's start at the root.

Your dick's base is where spongy erectile tissues connect to your pubic bone with some suspension ligaments—just south of the balls and north of the butthole. Go ahead and gently press on the spot. You can probably feel the spongy tissue under the skin.

The shaft of your dick is mostly composed of a spongy tissue called the *corpus cavernosum*. It's wrapped in a rigid sheath called the *tunica albuginea*. When you're not erect, blood flows into and out of your cock just as it circulates through your arms, legs, ears, and everything else. When someone whispers something delightfully dirty into your ear, or you lean against the washing machine during the spin cycle, you get aroused and your cock begins to stiffen.

This is when the muscles surrounding the blood vessels going into your dick relax, which allows blood to flow into the spongy tissues. At the same time, the muscles that control the outgoing blood flow constrict, which traps blood in the erectile tissues. When these tissues are engorged with blood and press against the hard sheath, your dick gets stiff.

The head of your penis is called the *glans*, and the part of the glans that flares out is called the *coronal ridge*, the little lip that runs along the bottom edge of the head. If you're uncircumcised, the foreskin is attached to the head at the corona, and if you're circumcised (approximately two thirds of American men are circumcised, and most of them are circumcised shortly after birth), well, that's where it used to be attached. But hey, there's no use crying over snipped skin, right?

The glans and corona have the most nerve endings in the penis—so, whether you're taking care of yourself of someone else, it makes sense to spend some good quality time there.

The *urethra* is the tube that runs the underside of your shaft and carries urine from the bladder and seminal fluid from the prostate. The *urethral opening* is the little hole at the tip of your cock head.

The *frenulum* is the bit of the penis real estate that runs from the urethral opening down the underside of your head. The skin seam that runs down from there is called the *raphe*. On some men it runs all the way over the testicles down to the anus. Both the frenulum and raphe are chock-full of nerve endings too.

Jumping ahead a little bit, let's talk about your orgasm. You may have thought your orgasm starts when you get your trick does that little circle-thing with his tongue, but physiologically speaking, it starts when your semen is forced into the urethra. This moment is called "ejaculatory inevitability," and it means there's no turning back. I like to call it: "Oh, my God—I'm gonna come!" It's less clinical.

Your balls retract, and your bladder entrance clamps shut so you don't urinate. The "uh !uh! yes! yes!" spasms are actually your urethra, prostate, perineum (see Secret #37) and penis contracting in a sequence called *peristalsis* to force the semen out of your body. (If you don't tell the sperm that they're not headed for an ovum, than neither will I.) You get about four good contractions—the kind that gets replayed in slow motion on vintage porn, then you get a few minor ones as well.

Like individual snowflakes, every orgasm is unique.

Some are a bang, and some are a whimper—it all depends on your anatomy and your age, not necessarily your level of arousal or excitement. Your partner may moan and groan so loudly when he gets close that you cover your eyes for fear he might put one of them out, but instead, he just dribbles out a few drops rather than erupting like a geyser. Just go with the flow (and maybe act like you were watching Old Faithful put on a show).

Discover the Miracle of Lube!

You uncircumcised readers—after reading Secret #12—can just whip it out and go to town on your Rumpleforeskin, no additional ingredients needed. Your foreskin acts like a little friction-reducing flesh tube, providing smooth sailing over the glans when you're masturbating. Circumcised guys, on the other hand, typically need a little motion lotion to prevent chapping and friction burns on their love wands. Thank goodness for personal lubricant. A miracle of modern science, lube comes in an amazing variety of textures and flavors, so you should definitely stock up on some.

When do you use it? It's optional for use on your own spam dagger when you're masturbating. Slippery is good, but not always totally necessary. But you must, must, *must* use it anytime you want to put a finger, a toy, or a cock in anyone's butt.

Aside from masturbating, lube is great for hand jobs, blow jobs, fucking, and also for advanced play such as fisting or the use of anal beads (though you should consider getting "industrial-strength" lubes made especially for those last two activities). Several kinds of lubricants are available at most drugstores these days, and you'll find even more at your local gay video shop or over the Internet. With so many choices available now, it makes sense to know a little bit about their uses, differences, and relative advantages and disadvantages.

Oil-based lubes are very slippery and are best when you're masturbating alone or with someone (or several someones). Because they erode latex, they're absolutely *not* to be used with condoms, dental dams, or latex gloves. They're good for all-over body massages as well, but don't use them internally unless it's for you and you alone. Don't do any prostate massages with this stuff, especially if you plan to fuck using condoms afterward. Oil-based lubes are incompatible with penetrative safe sex.

Water-based lubes come in a number of varieties, and some brands include a number of different flavors like grape, bubble gum, and green apple. They're great for giving head, since they provide a bit o' slickness when your salivary glands aren't getting the job done. They also come in handy when you need a little mental vacation. Going down on a hot man when his cock is piña colada-flavored can inspire a nice little tropical fantasy in midwinter. Water-based lubes are subject to evaporation and can dry out after a while, but a reapplication or a little rewetting with a few drops of water or spit can make the lubed area slick again. (Water-soluble lubes are not the same as water-based lubes, which may contain oils. Make sure you check the labels before buying.)

Silicone-based lubes won't erode condoms and other latex. They're safe to use on all your body parts, and they stay slick for ages. Ironically, they're not good for use with silicone toys, which tend to dissolve when in contact with silicone lube.

All these products are sold in various bottle- or tub-sizes, and they often come in single-serving packets as well—great for travel sex, or if you are experimenting and don't yet know which kind of lube you prefer. You should get your lube in tubes or bottles that squeeze, pump, or pour it out. A container into which you have to reach your hand can be a repository for germs and bacteria. You don't want to be sticking your hand into a petri dish and smearing critter-ridden goo all over your Mr. Bojangles.

But just because you can't get the drugstore doesn't mean you can't get slippery. There are a bunch of household products that will do the trick when you've just got to get off. Crisco is the great-granddaddy of household lubes. Just remember that Crisco, just like oil-based store-bought lubes (and vegetable oil, olive oil, mineral oil, peanut oil, etc.) eats away at latex and is a no-no for safe sex. Vaseline, baby oil, and hand lotions work for masturbation and massage. Buy the really cheap store-brand hand moisturizers, or Albolene, a brand of moisturizing cleanser—they're greasier and will stay slick longer.

Another makeshift lube that works in a pinch is hair conditioner, though it's best used in the shower. Stay away from anything with soap or alcohol in it like shampoo, bar or liquid soap, or shaving cream. These will dry out your cock—the skin may even flake off. Your johnson will eventually return to normal, but no one will want to go near it when it looks like a molting snake.

Another jerk-off don't comes from my friend Joe, 35, who said that once, as a young teenager, he used BenGay when jerking off. It was the first and last time he ever did that. He said it was the most painful sexual experience of his young life.

NO. 15 Practice, Practice, Practice

There are a few solo-masturbation techniques that, done at different speeds and in different positions, can produce orgasms of varying intensity. You've probably already got a favorite way to get your *petit mort* on, and I'm not here to tell you you're doing it wrong. If you like it and no one is getting hurt, it's cool with me. The key to enjoying yourself sexually is variation and experimentation.

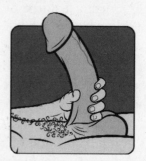

The **Basic Stroke** is to lie on your back in a comfortable spot and wrap your right hand (if you're right-handed; otherwise, use your left hand) around your erect cock and stroke up and down the shaft. You're saying "duh" to yourself right now, but I already told you this was the basic approach. The benefit of this approach is that you have a lot of skin-to-skin contact between your hand and your dick, and you'll stimulate a lot of nerves this way. While you've got one hand working on your cock, the other is free to tug gently on your balls, play with your asshole, squeeze your nipples, or fast-forward the porno flick with the remote control.

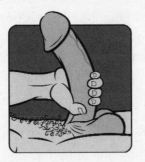

You can stroke off while standing, of course, or while you're kneeling or lying on your side. You can do this with your non-dominant hand (your left hand, if you're a righty) or with a **Backhand Grip.** The basic grip is when your hand is wrapped around your dick, with your thumb and forefinger at the top of your shaft while your pinkie is closer to your testicles. The backhand grip is when you rotate your wrist so that when your inverted hand is on your dick, your thumb and forefinger are closer to your balls and your pinkie finger is near the head. You may have to stroke to one side for this wank to work, but it does give you a different sensation than the basic grip.

The **Bed Bump** technique is when you use your whole body to simulate the motions of sex with a partner. Lie facedown on a bed or the floor. You can hold your erect cock in your motionless hand (or hands) and thrust your cock in and out of your fist to approximate fucking a little more closely than the basic approach. Try lying facedown with a pillow under your hips with silk sheets or with a soft, low-friction material under your dick. Trying this with flannel might result in a bed fire. You can also try this position with a condom that you've lubed on the inside and then slipped over your dick. The sensation is smoother and the cleanup is minimal. The added benefit is that learning to enjoy solo sex with a condom makes condom use more enjoyable with a partner.

To try the **Belly Rub** method, lie on your back and, with your hand extended flat (rather than in a grip), roll your lubed penis back and forth across your stomach. Try this by curling your fingers partway and stroke without encircling your cock with your hand. Try circular motions: back and forth, up and down. By rubbing your cock against your belly, you'll sense some different, perhaps new sensations, and new sensations are always good! You can also try this while you're lying facedown with your erect dick positioned on your belly and you're rocking your hips side-to-side.

For added pleasures, try a masturbation sleeve (available online or in sex shops); do it in front of a mirror (while playing Prince's "Sexy M.F." on your stereo); pick up a dirty magazine for inspiration; pop in a porno; or go step-by-step through that wild fantasy of yours—the one about the grocery store clerk, or about your hot neighbor who likes to wash his car with his shirt off.

NO. 16 How to Jerk Him Off

Now that you've got a good sense of the lay of the land, it's time to take matters into your own hands. Before attempting these jerk-off techniques on your trick or your beau (or yourself), make sure your hands are washed and that your nails are clean, trimmed, and filed. Anyone whose genitals have been on the receiving end of freshly chewed fingernail will understand the importance of smooth, clean nails. Please remove your watches, bracelets, and rings. Your class ring + his sensitive dick skin = nobody's good time.

Give his cock a good once-over look in decent light, especially if you've never been with him before. Ask about anything unusual, especially strange bumps, sores, or anything of the kind. It's better to get the story right now, if he hasn't mentioned any STDs. Most any guy will like the idea of your paying special attention to his wang—you don't have to tell him it's an inspection.

Get comfy by lying next to him, or by kneeling in front of him while he's sitting, or by facing him while straddling his lap with both your legs and his spread so you have room to move your hands. Make sure the room is warm enough—it's better to be a little too warm than too cold—you don't want his jewels shivering. Get your hands well-oiled and give these techniques a try!

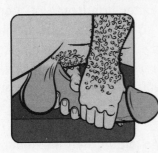

Double Stuff: This is just like the Basic Stroke, but with both hands wrapped around his cock. Gently slide both hands up and down together. The increased surface area of your skin touching his will feel fantastic.

The Pepper Mill: This is a variation on the Double Stuff. You twist each hand in a different direction on the upstroke, then in the opposite direction on the downstroke. Don't grip too tightly or twist too hard.

Love Tug: If your playmate isn't fully hard yet, try this two-handed technique—a variation on the Double Stuff in which you stroke in one direction. With one hand wrapped around his cock at the base, slide upward toward the head. When that hand is about to slide off, slide the other hand up from the same starting position.

Tunnel o' Love: Make a cylinder grip with your right hand and, beginning at the head, slide it over the head and all the way down the shaft with one hand. Do the same with your left hand, starting at the head as soon as your right hand has moved far enough down the shaft. Remove your right hand and repeat, keeping constant contact between your hands and his dick and maintaining constant motion, all in the downward direction. The sensation is like sliding his cock farther and farther into a mouth or ass in a state of perpetual penetration.

Jar Head: With one hand, encircle the base of his penis with your thumb and forefinger, then gently but firmly hold it in place. The ring your fingers are making will act like a cock ring, keeping his dick stiff and keeping it from flopping around. With the other hand out flat, perpendicular to his dick and your palm on the head of his penis, slowly and gently twist your hand side-to-side like you're opening a jar—maintaining contact with his cock all the while. The head of the penis is pretty sensitive, so he may smack your hand away quickly. But if he doesn't, he'll be squirming with joy.

Taffy Pull: The key to this technique, like the Tunnel o' Love, is constant hand-to-dick contact and fluidity of motion. Wrap one hand around the base of the shaft with an inverted grip and stroke upward. When you get to the head, cup your hand and fingers around the top. Slide one hand up and over the other, and then bring it back down the shaft with the standard grip. Before you open your grip, slide your other hand in an inverted grip again, up over your first hand and up the shaft. This one's a definite cock-pleaser.

Play-Doh Snake: Hold the shaft of his cock between your flattened palms. Gently move one hand to you and one hand away, then reverse, as if you were rolling out a snake made of Play-Doh. The skin at the sides of his shaft will gently twist back and forth. This is the same motion that Mr. Miyagi used to heal Ralph Macchio in *The Karate Kid*, though he wasn't grabbing Daniel-san's cock—and you'll want to omit the furious clap that preceded Mr. Miyagi's ministrations.

Thumb War: Facing him, gently grip him with both hands so that your thumbs line up next to each other on the underside of his cock on the raphe near the head. Steady his cock with your fingers on the other side while moving your thumbs in tiny circles or in opposite directions, back and forth, up and down.

Doorknob: This one's as simple as it sounds. Alternate your lubed hands, turning the head and shaft of the penis as if you were opening a door.

Try a few and ask him which ones he likes. Better yet, mix it up. Try the Doorknob then the Double Stuff. Try the Thumb War and the Play-Doh Snake then go back to Thumb War. Be adventurous!

NO. 17

Jizzer-cise

It always feels like a freight train rushing through your body when you're about to have an orgasm. But it doesn't always look as impressive as it feels. If you consider your orgiastic output less than an impressive display, feel free to place the blame on porn.

I'm a big fan of porn, personally, and I love to incorporate it into sexual experiences. But porn must be taken for what it is: a fantasy depiction of sex. It's not real-life sex. It's like those fat-free chocolate cookies. They're not *really* food, but sometimes we mistake them for the real thing.

Sadly, many of us gay and bi men look at porn as though it were a step-by-step manual for gay sex, and as the yardstick by which we should measure our bodies and those of our partners. Granted, you can pick up a hint or two or indulge a fantasy by watching porn, but a porn film is not a visual how-to manual. Porn simply is not the standard against which to evaluate your body, cock size, or the distance you shoot your load.

Using porn to judge yourself and your sexual response can be very frustrating. Porn star dicks are not average size (average size of an erect penis is between five and six inches, depending on which scientific study you consult). Porn model bodies are not average bodies. There's a reason these guys are in porn: They have great bodies, they often have big dicks, and they're okay with having sex with a lot of people watching. And, through the magic of editing and Viagra, they have the benefit of looking like sex gods.

Unless you live in Southern California, you most likely

won't be dating porn stars. Still, there are a few tricks of the trade that we can adopt to enhance our sexual experiences. My friend Sonny dated a porn star for a very brief stint. And while he said the sex with Ben the Bottom (not his real name) was great, he also learned a few pointers that he's since used in sex with other guys—for example, how to increase the volume of his ejaculate. (It's fascinating what friends will tell you when you're writing a sex book.) BB's tips were to drink a lot of water, hold off from ejaculating for several days, and make your sex sessions last a nice long time. When you finally come, your money shot will be more impressive. Just you try waiting several days to come, though. My informal research subjects would take several good orgasms over just one impressive money shot any day.

While it's nice to put on a good show, remember that it's far more important that your orgasm feels good. A very small urethral opening tends to produce more pressure and therefore a more powerful splooge stream. Like closing off part of a garden hose with the water running, the smaller opening increases the water pressure, making the water shoot farther. And even guys who can shoot across the room will notice the power of their ejaculate decreasing with age. It's natural. That's the way the fat-free cookie crumbles.

Delay Tactics
Imagine it: you've got a hot guy in your bed, and he's doing everything right.

Tongues and hands in all the right places, cocks and asses making sweet music together—you're close to coming, but you really don't want it to end yet. What do you do? Do you start thinking about baseball statistics or Barbara Bush in a sting bikini to keep from coming? Turning your thoughts to a total turnoff topic may have been your grandfather's approach (even way back when your grandpa was a horny teenager, Barbara was still a wood-deflator), but we young'uns know better now.

Instead of taking your head out of the game, stay in the zone by paying attention to your body's responses and using them to delay orgasm until you're good and ready. But before we get into the subtle messages that your body is sending you—telling you your cock is about to throw out some thin white ropes—let's chat about the kind of shape your equipment needs to be in to get the most mileage. Here's where one of the beneficial side effects of masturbation comes in handy: muscle tone.

While choking the chicken won't give you six-pack abs, it will tone up your pubococcygeus (PC) muscle, which is partly responsible for controlling your orgasm. The PC muscle is the one that you contract to stop the flow of urine. It's also the muscle that, if contracted when you're erect, makes your cock jump. Get to know this muscle. Make it your friend. Strengthening it and learning to control it will make your erections firmer and your ejaculations more powerful, plus you'll be able to delay ejaculation for much longer than you could with little girlie PC muscles.

To strengthen it, try **Kegel exercises** (named for Arnold Kegel, the physician who developed the technique) by squeezing the muscle that you use to stop the flow of urine when you're taking a leak—except do it when you're not taking a leak, such as when you're driving or watching TV or in a meeting at work. Contract the muscle for 10 seconds and release, then rest for 10 seconds. Then go again, gradually increasing the length of time and number of contractions. You can do this exercise anywhere, because even when you're doing it, no one can tell by looking at you. The PC muscle is a quick healer, so in a few weeks time you'll be waking up in the morning with stiffer stiffies. During sex, you can contract the PC muscle to control your ejaculatory inevitability.

Another delay tactic that regular masturbation can help you master is the **start-stop technique**. When you're jerking off and about to come, just before you reach the point of no return, let go of your wood, relax, breathe deeply, and wait until the orgasmic feeling subsides. Then go to town again. Repeat until your arm gives out. Pay attention to the stimulus that sends you over the edge, and practice controlled breathing and relaxation until you can feel yourself teetering on that big-O edge for longer and longer periods of time.

Another method is the **squeeze technique,** whereby you wrap two fingers around your penis, just under the head, and give it a good firm squeeze when you're almost about to come. Hang on to this grip until the orgasmic sensations subside, then resume your carnal activities.

Whatever method you use, do not rub desensitizing or anesthetic creams onto your penis. They're designed to keep you from feeling anything, and they're bad because, well, *they keep you from feeling anything.*

NO. 19

Injaculation

While this book is too short to go into the finer points of the sexual techniques of Eastern cultures, injaculation is a method that is popular among many practitioners, and unlike Tantric sex, which can take years to master, it's easily learned in one or two stroke sessions.

Injaculation is the practice of using external pressure to prevent the expulsion of semen from the penis. The purpose in Taoist philosophies is to prevent valuable life energy from escaping your body, as Taoists believe it does every time you shoot your wad. For non-Taoists, injaculation or (retrograde ejaculation) is a practice that can lead to a shorter refractory period (the downtime between coming and being ready for action again). Some folks claim it can also help you experience more intense orgasms.

During normal ejaculation, semen passes through the urethra from the prostate and shoots out the urethral opening at the tip of your dick. The urethra tube runs in the area between your balls and anus, the perineum, also known as the "taint." ('T'aint your balls, and 't'aint your ass) Cop a feel downtown, and you'll be able to find the spot on the taint that Western Taoists call the "million-dollar point" just before the anus. It's got a spongy feel to it, primarily because it's also the inner end of the *corpus spongiosum*, the erectile tissue that runs the length of your penis.

You can prevent ejaculation by pressing firmly on the money spot. Immediately before orgasm, press down into the spongy area with one index finger on the point, and use your middle finger and ring finger to hold it in place. Keep your fingers still until your orgasm has stopped. If you've done it right, you reached orgasm but didn't ejaculate. No muss, no fuss!

By preventing ejaculation, you may have redirected the seminal fluid into the bladder, which sounds bad, but shouldn't pose a health problem if you allow yourself plenty of unimpeded "regular" orgasms as well. You'll notice that your urine might be a little cloudy when you pee after trying this. If you're willing to give this a try, think of it as an occasional practice—once in a while won't cause any harm. However, you don't want too much unexpelled semen building up; there are potential health risks involved in that. Also, be gentle with your urethra. Too much pressure or regularly repeated pressure can lead to health problems as well. The taint is not designed to withstand high pressures regularly.

Regular practitioners stay erect and can go again almost immediately after an injaculation, and many of them say that their orgasms are different in sensation. For masturbators, this can mean a pleasurable and extended flog-the-bishop session. During sex with another person, injaculation might just mean you can hump like the Energizer Bunny for hours and hours and hours...

NO. 20 Diddle Don'ts

We've covered a few things you should do with your dick and a few things you should do with his. Here are a few masturbation warnings your mama would have given you—if she had no sense of appropriate child-parent boundaries:

★ Don't try to make your cock bigger. Penis pumps, herbal treatments: They're all a crock. There are penis-lengthening surgeries where the doctor cuts the suspensory ligaments that make your cock jump when you flex your PC muscles. Once the ligaments are cut, the dick hangs a bit lower than before, but it is not actually any longer—and you can't ever make it jump again!

★ Never put anything up your butt that could get lost because of its shape. If you like to wear a butt plug while you masturbate, make sure it's got a flared base. Stay away from candles, cucumbers, or anything that could slip inside and not come out. Nobody ever got off from having a doctor remove an embarrassing item from his anus. If you had the balls to buy this book, then you have the balls to get yourself a hands-free butt plug.

★ Don't put your cock anywhere that it might get stuck. Despite the obvious erotic allure of the vacuum cleaner, it is a bad, bad idea to shake your moneymaker anywhere near it. There are fan blades in there! Even if the hose attachment appears to be a great fit for your penis, just stay the hell away. It can pull the skin right off your tool.

★ Don't stick your dick into anything made of glass. That soda bottle or flower vase might look like it's the perfect size, and even if it was the right size when you stuck it in, your dick could swell and seal off the entrance, creating a painful and dangerous vacuum inside the bottle. Cracking or smashing the glass to break the vacuum could mean serious cuts on your willy.

★ Don't cook your cock by subjecting it to extreme heat. If you want to stroke off with those heat pads designed to reduce muscle pain or zipper bag full of warm oatmeal (people do it!), then make sure whatever you're using is cool enough to hold in your hand for 30 seconds.

★ Don't try puppetry of the penis when you're erect. Trying to bend your penis too far in any direction can actually fracture your little friend. Such fractures can result in Peyronie's disease (curved dick disease).

CHAPTER 3

Seduction and "Foreplay"

★★

NO. 21

Maintain the Seduction Momentum—While You're Still Clothed

The hot guy from the bar or the party or the Laundromat is sitting on your couch. (What was his name—William or Sam or something like that? You can check his driver's license later.) He's looking at your coffee-table books, and you're in the kitchen getting him something to drink. Nice work, kiddo! Your confidence, your seductive body language, and honest, direct flattery sealed the deal—well, almost.

Moving from the meeting place to the couch in your living room is a major step, but it can take you out of the seductive moment, and that can interrupt your mojo's momentum. In every other episode of *Sex and the City*, that slut Samantha tumbles through her front door, her bra undone and her leg wrapped around the bare ass of some hunky guy. You may find that most trips back to your place with a new beau simply do not unfold in quite such a dramatic way. It probably took a few minutes to get home, and chances are that the heat of the moment—that great, steamy, spine-tingling moment when you decided to go home together—has diminished a little in the intervening minutes. Maybe you kissed a little bit at the bar; maybe you rubbed your hand over his chest and under his T-shirt when you were going to your cars or the subway. Or maybe you didn't, and you're waiting for the right moment—here, at your place (or there at his). The moment to make your move is now. Make him remember it!

Stop! Before you go any further, if you're hosting the little rendezvous, give yourself and your place a quick once-over. Check your breath (mints are okay, but you don't want to be chomping on gum if he goes in for the kill before you do). Adjust the lighting to its optimal sex-conducive setting—low but not so dark that you're tripping over your furniture. Music is good too. Pick something you like, obviously, but nothing that will put him to sleep.

Hand him his drink and make sure your hands touch a little bit. If you were talking, that's great—keep talking, especially if he's funny or if he's laughing at your jokes. If you weren't talking, tell him you make the most fantastic caipirinhas and he'll have to come back sometime to have one. (Then make a mental note to learn how to mix a caipirinha.)

The worst thing that can happen now is for you to sit back and let the polite chitchat turn into a long, polite conversation. Long conversation, especially after you've been out having a few drinks, can be the kiss of death for a hookup. You don't want to get bored, and you don't want him to change his mind about having come over. Do something. Make a move. Don't wait too long. Seduce him.

Seduction is about knowing what you want, making him feel like he's the only thing you want, and displaying the confidence to go get what you want. (See the pattern? It's about what *you* want. If you want him and you let him know it, it can be a very strong aphrodisiac, and he'll respond accordingly).

But how? Make eye contact or make physical contact—or both at the same time. Put one hand on his thigh and, with your other hand, take his drink from his hand and set it down on the coffee table. Then just lean forward and kiss him. Or unbutton the top button of his shirt and touch the skin underneath. Just make sure you make a move—don't wait.

NO. 22 Make Out Like a Teenager Again

Kissing is a magic thing. It expresses lust, tenderness, intimacy, and animalistic desires—all at once. It's an act of vulnerability and bonding. And it's so hot! Kissing styles are infinite in their variety: a tender kiss, a gentle bite on your lover's lip, a passionate openmouthed kiss when you're grabbing at each other's bodies. Fresh breath is a necessity, so brush your teeth (and tongue) regularly, and keep some mints handy. Lip balm can keep your lips nice and soft, but don't apply immediately before the smooching. He'll enjoy working on your joystick, but spare him from eating your ChapStick.

A book is hardly the place to learn how to kiss properly. It's a matter of practice, practice, practice. Still, there are some pitfalls that my crack team of experts (my homo friends, after a few drinks) has compiled into a brief list. Kissing is personal, and each guy likes his smooch sessions a little different, but there are a few things you shouldn't do unless you've got very clear indications he's into them.

Don't slobber all over his face, and keep the drool to a minimum. Yes, they do slobber all over each other in some pornos featuring the heavily-tattooed and pierced guys, and the guys being drooled on act as if they're receiving manna from heaven. But again, a porn film is not a sex manual; it's an idealized depiction of a specific fantasy. There's nothing wrong with a little spit if you're both into it, but until you know he likes it, hold back. Most guys don't like drool drying on their faces while they're macking. Wait for your partner to say, "whaddya say we slobber all over each other?"

Don't lunge at him as if you're trying to reenact those movie-magic moments when two star-crossed lovers dart at each other openmouthed and madly, passionately start making out. Yes, it can happen in real life, but the risk of chipping a tooth is kind of high. Besides, you risk looking like a fish at feeding time. Possible exceptions include your partner saying, "You know, I love those romantic movies where they lunge at each other." Give it a practice run first.

Don't start out your make-out session with your tongue swirling around in his mouth like an outboard motor blade. Tongue action is something you have to work up to, even if you've worked up to it after only a moment. It's okay to start slow, then work up to openmouthed kissing and tongue action.

Tense, dry kisses aren't much fun either. Relax!

Sex is both mental and physical, so make sure you pay attention to and enjoy the sensations you're giving each other. Kiss his neck, kiss his earlobes, and gently bite his lips. Your lips have a lot of sensitive nerve endings too, so tickling and teasing the lips can send some nice chills down his spine. Put your mouth as close to his as possible without actually kissing. Brush your lips very gently across his. Try this for a minute and see who dives in for the kiss first.

When you're kissing, give your hands something to do too, whether they're grabbing his ass, teasing his nipples through his shirt, stroking his hair, gently grabbing his head and pulling him into you, or pulling him off the couch so you can roll around on the floor with your bodies pressed together. Having a lot of body-to-body contact when you're still clothed can be a great anticipation-builder. If it feels this good when clothed, image what it will be like when you're both naked.

Word to the wise: Be wary of men who won't kiss. Any man who is ready to fuck you but won't kiss you is likely to be really uncomfortable with being gay. Some men just prefer not to kiss, but it's often the result of years of antigay social programming or internalized homophobia or self-loathing. A lot of these men think that they can have butt sex with guys, but if they don't kiss, it means they're not gay. That's bullshit, and you might as well stay away.

NO. 23 Forget About Foreplay

Forget about foreplay? That's what I said! Foreplay—as it's most often discussed in *Maxim* or *GQ* or wherever—is a term that applies primarily to straight people. The stages of arousal for women are different than they are for men, so foreplay is based on the idea that men have to work with a woman's stages of arousal. To put a finer point on it, she needs to get wet and into the mood, and foreplay is how that happens.

Personally, I ain't unhooking nobody's bra. And if you're reading this book, chances are you aren't either. Forget those foreplay rules. Men have an *on* switch. It's not hard to find, and when it's on, it's on. You don't usually have to warm us up to get into the mood for sex. We're already hardwired for it (and a lot of us are just plain constantly hard for it). When two men get together for sex, you don't have think in terms of first base, second base, third base, or home run.

In heterosexual sex, vaginal intercourse is the home run. Not so for us. If you want to, you can go to third base before you get to second. Do it all, mix it up, in any order you like. You can make out after you've gone down on each other; you can massage each other after you've rimmed him or stroked his cock. There's no strict procedure, so if you feel like doing something, you should do it, and you shouldn't be worried about whether you're doing it in the right order. If you're having a good time, then you're doing it in the right order.

That said, it's definitely worth taking the time to work a

man into a hormonal delirium. You don't have to dive for his cock right away. You can take your time here—go slow, make him beg for it. Take the one-button-at-a-time approach to undressing.

Speaking of which, it's about time you moved into the bedroom—if that's where you want to be. After all, you can do each other right there on the couch if you like. But before you screw, you should screw the old rules you learned about sex.

NO. 24 Make Him Putty in Your Hands

If you haven't totally ditched your clothes on the way to the bedroom, you might consider giving him a little striptease, or even asking for him to do the same for you. If you've got even the tiniest exhibitionist streak in you, then stand up while he lies down on the bed and ask him which piece of clothing you should take off. He'll suggest something, and you'll do it. You can make him match you, article for article, until you're both buck-naked. If he's got an exhibitionist streak, you can find out pretty quickly by asking him to do a little striptease for you. If he's into it—and a lot of guys are—he'll get turned on by revealing himself for you.

Nervous about stripping for him? It helps to have the right kind of music playing. It's damn near impossible to strip to Enya or Kenny G. (well, not impossible, but really dull), but if you're shedding clothes to a little sexy soul, or some hot and funky pop music—even that old standby

Barry White—he'll be popping right out of his shorts while you're dropping yours to the floor.

If you're not feeling the *Showgirls* vibe, and you want to remove clothing in a more traditional manner, just massage him right out of his togs. Start with him sitting, facing away from you while you massage his shoulders, neck, and mid back from a sitting position. Everyone loves getting a good massage, and the massager gets the pleasure of running his hands all over his partner's body. Start by pressing your thumbs gently into the muscles on either side of the spine in medium-size circles. Don't press too firmly on the spine. Now is a good time to suggest that if he removed his shirt and pants the massage would feel better.

Personally, I think it's only fair for the massager to remove the same amount of clothing as the one getting the massage. It's so unfair that professional masseurs at most legit day spas don't feel the same way. Once his shirt and pants are off, have him lie facedown on the bed. Take care to run your hands all over his back, shoulders, arms, buttocks, and legs—even his feet, if he's not too ticklish. (And if he is, make a mental note and file it away for later torment—I mean, use.)

Anyone who's had a really great massage knows there's a chance you'll become so relaxed that you'll fall asleep. Compound a good back rub with the cocktails he had at the bar and the one you fed him when you got him to your place, and the effect can be narcotic. Keep the massage relatively short and sweet and deliver a few well-placed licks, kisses, and gentle bites when you're giving the massage—they'll keep him awake and hard as a rock.

Also consider trying some massage oils that heat up when you use them. There are a few varieties that are edible and nonstaining, just like water-based lube, so you don't have to worry about licking him all over after the massage. Otherwise, make sure he's lying on a towel or sheet you don't mind getting stained.

NO. 25 Discover the Pleasures of Putting on a Show

Watching your partner masturbate and touch his own body are great ways for you to pick up tips on how he likes to be stroked and touched. Once you're both naked and hard, move a few feet away from him and watch him as each of you strokes his dick. Keep your eyes on him, not your stiffy. Two things are most likely to happen: (1) He will get up and move closer to you. No problem there—continue playing as you were. (2) He will lie back and watch you as you stroke yourself. Study how he holds his cock—does he like fast pumping or long, slow strokes? See if he plays with his balls—does he tug on them, or roll them around in his hand? Watch to see if he fingers his ass or squeezes his nipples. He knows what he likes done to his body, and he can tell you without ever saying a word.

There's a principle called the Golden Rule of Sex: Do unto him what you want him to do unto you. It's a simple idea, and it works both ways. Whatever he does to you is probably the kind of thing he likes to have done to him. Mutual masturbation is a great way to test this theory. Pay attention to what he does to you when he's jerking you off. Does he nibble your earlobes, nuzzle your neck, or play with your butt? There's a good chance that if you do the same stuff to him, he'll love it. Give him the same nonverbal cues too: If you really want him to tug on your nipples, then give his a little squeeze. He'll probably get the picture.

If you're getting crossed signals—for example, he plays with your balls but won't let you touch his—just ask. Gay men tend to be fairly explicit about what they like to do and have done to them in bed. Asking "You like this?" is usually enough to get a very clear answer.

NO. 26 Keep Him in the Dark

The opposite of watching each other is not being able to see anything at all. Sex in the dark can produce all kinds of different and new sensations. Darkness can add a bit of zing to a hard-core scene, and it can do the same for a tamer coupling. Without sight, you're left with the sound of his voice and the feel of his body. You can shed any insecurity about the way you look, whose type you think you appear to be, or how you'll look when you're having sex. Sex in the dark is somehow less mannered and more animalistic—which accounts for the popularity of back rooms in clubs.

A darkened room lit only by a little moonlight or by a candle—or a totally dark room where neither of you can see anything at all—can really kick your play into high gear. Besides the potential for setting a romantic mood (which is nice, occasionally), turning off the lights can be a big turn-on for a lot of men, primarily because it means eliminating our primary source of sexual sensory input: our sight. Men are very visually oriented. By turning off that part of your sensory array, you can heighten other senses that are often neglected in sex play: smell, hearing, and touch.

To put one rather than both playmates in the dark, consider using a blindfold. While hoods and zipper masks are great for kinky scenes, a simple handkerchief, scarf, or even a sleep mask can provide the necessary sensory depravation for non-S/M sex.

Dax, 31, and Greg, 33, are a couple who live in Denver. They've done plenty of sexy stuff together, including having three-ways and tying each other up. But after four years together they'd never once used a blindfold. Dax talks about Greg's blindfolding him with a handkerchief for the first time one night: "The fact that we'd never done it before was fun. I didn't know what Greg would do next. The anticipation got me really wound up. But the most amazing part of it to me was how heightened every other sense was. I could smell and hear everything so much more vividly—and the smell of his body was so hot. Having him touch me all over felt totally new and really erotic. It was hot to know that Greg was in total control too, and I totally let go."

Blindfolding works best if the players trust each other, since one player will be at the mercy of the other one—even if you fear that the worst he can do is tickle you. But if the blindfolded man can easily take off the blindfold when he chooses, it doesn't really matter if you've had sex before or if he's a first-time date. No blindfold handy? You can also approximate some of the heightened sensory play if you ask your partner to close his eyes. With his peepers out of commission, amp up his sense of smell by using scented massage oils (if you don't plan to have sex that involves latex) or incense. Give him goose bumps all over by tickling his body with feathers or fuzzy gloves—even your hot breath on his skin can feel over-the-top incredible. Use your hands to gently stroke and tickle your partner's body until he's all aquiver with pleasure.

No. 27 Erogenous Zones, Part I: Nips 'n' Pits

The nipples are like the Holy Grail for many gay men, and a little know-how in nipple play can send a nipple-sensitive man up like a rocket. The nipples are loaded with tons of nerve endings, and during arousal the nipples receive an increased flow of blood, making them even more sensitive. Some men have nipples that swell and become erect during arousal. As with any erogenous zone, some kinds of stimulation work on some guys but not on others. Some guys like gentle play, others like rougher play, and some like none at all.

Nipples are little, but they can be mighty responsive. Try licking them, gently pinching them, sucking them, or rubbing a fingertip over them when they've been moistened with spit. Using tit clamps (little metal clips that fit on each nipple and are often connected by a chain for easy one-handed tugging) or gently playing with nipple piercings can enhance tit play. Some men find that the more they play with their nipples, the more they enjoy it and the more sensitive their nipples become.

Brad, a 26-year-old San Diego bartender, has always

had sensitive nipples. But getting his nipples pierced, he says, was "installing a hotline to my groin." He encourages tricks to play with his piercings during sex, and he often plays with them when he's masturbating.

If your playmate is playing with your nipples, give him some clues to let him know that he's giving you the right amount of pressure, or that he's giving you a little too much. Any guy who is into heavier nipple play or tit torture will probably be happy to tell you exactly what he likes. Ask him to show you what to do!

Armpits are another highly eroticized spot on the male form. As with nipples (and feet and butts) some men are into armpits; others prefer to keep them out of sight and out of mind. But anyone who has been tickled under the arms knows the sensitive nature of that bit of body geography.

Especially in North America, the sight of hair under the arms is a total masculinity signifier—mainly because most women (and many androgynous male fashion models) keep their underarms shaved. Some men are attracted by the taboo nature of armpits. After all, there is a whole industry established to make sure they stay hairless and/or odorless. The continuum of tastes runs from men who like freshly showered pits to those who like them superstinky. Most guys who are into smelly pits are the kind who will tell you straight up that they like you ripe, not shower-fresh. For these guys, remember to leave the deodorant and antiperspirant behind—they'll leave a nasty aftertaste on his tongue.

As with most sexual experiences, diving into the armpits takes a sense of adventure and a willingness to try new experiences. If your partner likes pits, then nuzzle his pits, sniff them, lick them, and ask him to do the same for you— you'll send your guy into orbit.

No. 28

Erogenous Zones, Part II: Tush to Toes

Touched properly, the entire human body can become one big erogenous zone, but there are a few spots below the waist (aside from the family jewels) that deserve a little special attention: the butt, legs, and feet.

Ask a gay man whether he's an ass man, and he knows right away. Aside from being the gate to heavenly bliss, the tush is a thing of beauty, whether clothed or naked, or semi-clothed in a pair of sexy briefs, a jockstrap, or boxers. You don't have to be a top to appreciate a nice fuzzy crack or a round, perfectly hairless bubble butt. And butt play needn't always mean playing inside the anus. A great massage on the glutes can be incredibly arousing. Aside from fucking, you can also kiss, lick, and of course spank the posterior.

Likewise, the inner thighs and the backs of the knees are great places to run your tongue, kiss, or nibble. Both areas are spots that don't get much contact in day-to-day life, and that simple fact makes them the perfect parts of your man to explore.

A few basic massage techniques can help you make the most of your contact with these parts. If you're using massage oils or lotions, put the lotion in your hand and rub it to warm it up. The sudden splash of cool oil on a warm back can be an unpleasant shock and can result in schlong shrinkage. Love-buzz kill! You don't want his balls retracting into his body cavity while you rub him down.

Start with light strokes that follow the contours of his limbs and muscles before you go in for deeper massaging. Professional massage therapists know that long strokes are relaxing while quick strokes and rubbing are invigorating. Unless you're a pro, stick with the relaxing kind. Pros will also tell you that deep strokes in therapeutic massage should be directed toward the heart. In the case of sensual massage, the strokes should be directed toward the genitals for maximum arousal.

Whole books have been written about men's obsession with feet. Foot and shoe fetishes are among the most common kinks for men, gay and straight. Regardless of whether you're into feet as an object of worship, pay heed: The feet, especially the soles, are just brimming with sensitive nerve endings. If you like toe-sucking, then get to it! But you may want to avoid the massage oils on the feet. He'll tell you if toe-to-tongue action doesn't float his boat.

Gently massage one foot, then the other. Start with the top of the foot, make strokes the full length of the foot, then move in to work your thumbs gently into the spaces between the tendons. If the pressure is too light, the sensation will feel like tickling, and you may end up with a few teeth missing when he accidentally kicks you in the face. For the soles of the feet, move your thumbs in small circles from the base of the toes to the heel, then pay attention to each individual toe, stroking and gently twisting from base to tip.

Get Your Mojo Rising: Talking Dirty

Joel, a 30-year-old film industry executive in Los Angeles, told me about a vacation to Budapest, where he met a tall, dark, Eastern European hot-tie in a club.

"This hot guy didn't speak any English, and I didn't speak Hungarian, but we were definitely into each other. So after some hand gestures and writing down addresses, he indicated that he'd be interested in coming back to my hotel with me. We're in my room and we're have a totally great, totally wordless time when all of a sudden he breaks out with 'You like my big dick? Oh, yeah, suck my big dick!'—in perfect porno English! I had to try really hard to keep from bursting out laughing. Luckily, my mouth was busy."

While the Hungarian's heart was in the right place (he was engaged in he best kind of international diplomacy I can think of), dirty talk during sex—and even before sex—too often devolves into conventional porno-speak. Some guys prefer no talking during sex, while others like a non-stop dialogue about what feels good, whether to go harder or faster, the weather—anything. The trick is to find a happy medium where a little suggestive smut revs a guy up.

Try something that refers specifically to you, and to him—and avoid detached phrases that can easily sound canned or refer to disembodied parts. Instead of "Suck that dick," try "I love having my whole cock down your throat." Instead of "Gimme that fat cock," try "Your dick feels so great in my ass." Make your dirty talk direct and specific.

A little dirty talk before the main event, especially in an unexpected situation, can get a potential partner's juices flowing too. Say you're with a date (or someone you just met) at a black-tie fund-raiser. Lean close and say, "I would love to see you bent over and taking my cock while you're wearing nothing but that tie," or "I'd love to blow you in the bathroom right now." Then smile and look around the room as though you'd just been discussing the silent auction. Just be prepared to follow through if he takes you up on the offer.

More detailed dirty talk can involve your collection of toys ("I want you to use that vibrator all over me tonight"); bondage ("I'm going to tie you up and slap my hard cock all over your body, and you're going to love it!"); or your fantasies ("Do you know what the punishment is for driving over the speed limit, son?"). Bear in mind that some scenes take a little working up to—if you're gonna start calling him "bitch," test the waters a bit first before starting your dirty talk full tilt.

NO. 30 Aye, There's the Rub

Plenty of guys think the only real gay sex is mouth-to-penis, or mouth-to-anus, or penis-to-anus action. That's as ridiculous as saying the only purpose of sex is reproduction. We're living, breathing, humping proof that sex is a hell of a lot of fun, even if we're not reproducing. There are fun and games aplenty for nonpenetrators, including frottage.

Frottage is the old-school term for rubbing up against someone. Sexually speaking, it usually refers to full-body, cock-to-cock rubbing, where one guy is on top of the other. Frottage is common as a first sexual experience with another person—and with good reason: There's no penetration required and very little in terms of precision technique to be mastered. You just rub whatever of yours up against whatever of his—and voilá! It's sometimes called the "Princeton belly rub," in commemoration of all those college guys who at one time or another, lay naked atop one another and rubbed their lubed cocks together to get off. (I won't say anything more about their alleged heterosexuality, except that I'm glad the lads were experimenting.)

One mode of frottage is a great alternative to anal sex: Interfemoral intercourse is the fancy name for sticking your dick between his thighs and humping. Because of the proximity to the ass and because skin-on-skin contact is damn hot, this kind of frottage is a good alternative to butt sex when neither party wants to get fucked. Put some lube on your cock, have him hold his legs tightly together, and slide in. Try this technique lying or standing, positioned face-to-face, or facing the same way. Anyone into butts will still be able to rub his erection between some buns, and you can switch roles in a split second.

Another benefit of frottage is that it's a low-risk activity in terms of STDs—just be sure to keep ejaculate away from anuses and urethras.

CHAPTER 4

Cock and Ball Tips

★★★

NO. 31

Convertibles vs. Hardtops

You've got Mr. Wonderful home and on your couch or on your bed. You've stripped for him, and now he's stripping for you. He gets down to his cute 2(x)ist boxer briefs, and—Oh, my God! That's not what you thought his package would look like. His chorizo is uncut. Just roll with it, chief. There's very little difference between guys who are circumcised and those who aren't when it comes to sucking and fucking. If you've only been with snipped guys and never blown a guy who is intact, or if you've got a tube steak with a turtleneck and you've never stroked off a guy with a crewneck cock, relax and enjoy the experience! You can learn what you need to know below.

About two-thirds of the men in the United States are circumcised, but the percentage is significantly lower in the rest of the world, especially Europe, Asia, and South America. Aside from making your cock kosher, the main reasons most people now have their baby boys circumcised is simply that it's common practice or that they prefer the aesthetics of a circumcised dick. Parents don't want their boys to look different in the showers after gym class.

The medical establishment has changed its mind on the procedure a few times since the 1970s, so you'll probably be seeing the ratio of cut versus uncut evening out a bit. Personally, I love the variety, in or out of the showers. Because we're such highly evolved creatures, we homos can see how alluring both kinds of cocks are, and we know better than to write off a potential partner simply because his helmet wears a hoodie (or doesn't).

Contrary to myth, an uncut dick is not a dirtier dick. Though secretions may build up just under the head of uncut penises, you can easily clean the head by retracting the foreskin and washing it with soap and water. So long as everyone—both cut and uncut—washes his johnson on a daily basis, there's nothing to worry about in terms of cleanliness. (Besides, scrubbing up is just a nice thing to do if you're planning to play naked with others.) In a similar vein, health professionals once thought that guys with café curtains were more susceptible to fungal and urinary tract infections, but the jig is up—hoodless guys are at no less health risk for these infections than hooded.

Uncut guys often have the luxury of being able to rub one out without the aid of lubricant. The extra skin gives the cock a handy glide function and because the foreskin (which can almost cover the head or can dangle up to an inch below the tip of the dick) holds in precome and helps to keep the head slick.

Uncut dicks may be more sensitive because the foreskin covers the glans and keeps it from routinely rubbing against your jockeys. Cut guys have no protective sheath, so their dickheads become gradually less sensitive. Thus, when the foreskin on uncut cocks retracts, the glans is usually more sensitive to the touch.

Applying a condom is the same for both cut and uncut tools, except that the foreskin on uncut dicks should be retracted before rolling the rubber on. And when erect, there's very little difference between the two varieties in terms of function. A rose is a rose is a rose, right? If anyone asks about you about yours, offer to show him. If the man stripping at the foot of your bed asks you how yours works, give a little tutorial.

Blow Job Boot Camp

How difficult can it be to give a blow job? Open mouth, insert cock, and bob head up and down, right? Not so fast, Mister! That's how accidents happen. Let's move back a step or two. Giving great head is an art, not a science, and a lot of the art of giving head is actually in your head—the upstairs one. It doesn't matter if you imagine yourself as the gay Don Juan or as a boy-toy sex slave—you need to get your head into the head-giving game. If you decide you're the greatest cocksucker to walk

(crawl, writhe) across this earth, then you're probably
going to give one hell of a great blow job. And since your
attitude is contagious, he will love the fact that you're so
into it when you go downtown on him. He'll quiver, hearing that you're his sex god, and he's going to get the benefit of all your attention.

So you're not the world's greatest cocksucker? Don't
worry. We don't pop out of the womb ready to start giving
blow jobs. It's an acquired skill, but desire is lesson number
one: If you tell yourself you're the best goddamned cocksucker in town, you'll feel like it, and you'll stand a fighting
chance of becoming the world champ (what would those
Olympics be like?).

Oral sex is an opportunity, not an obligation. We love
dick, and we love sucking dick. It's our privilege as fag-
gots to worship dick (and have our wands worshipped
too). Worried about what it looks like when you've got
his schlong in your mouth? From the vantage point of the
receiver, the sight of your lips wrapped around his piece
is a sight more beautiful than any Caravaggio painting. It's
super hot, and the more you look like you love doing it, the
hotter it will look to him. Add to that some eye contact—
looking him in the eye when you're going down on him—
and he might just cream just from stimulus overload.

Desire? Check. The next BJ lesson is a biggie: Careful
with the teeth. If you're worried about accidentally scraping your teeth on his cock when you're sucking on him,
you can curl your lips over your teeth as though you were
imitating an old, toothless person. Lips feel good on your
cock, so consider that a beginner's technique that can be
modified when you are comfortable with the idea of him
sliding his cock in and out of your mouth. When you're

cool with the grandpa approach, do your best Angelina Jolie imitation and purse your lips out on front of your choppers so that they're in constant contact with his dick. Simultaneously open your mouth a little wider but keep your tongue and cheeks in contact with his cock. It's all about surfaces, honey.

Teeth and lips in check? On to lubrication. Since he'll be sliding in and out of your mouth, you're going to want to make his dick nice and slick. Be sure you're mustering as much saliva as you can. Use a lot, maybe use a little more than you think you need since it dries pretty quickly. Trust me, unlike when you're making out, he won't mind a little slobber here. Keep a glass of water nearby to remedy a dry mouth, and keep that tube of lube handy too. Lube can be a great BJ asset; it can help you give him that smooth sliding sensation. Coming up for air and a sip of water will also give your jaw a rest. Don't worry, you'll be building those muscles up in no time, and they'll catch up with your PC muscles soon enough. You'll be able to crush walnuts with 'em.

If he's uncut, you can use your mouth to slide his foreskin up and down the shaft of his cock, but you'll eventually want to use a couple of fingers (bonus points if you can use your tongue) to retract the foreskin to expose the supersensitive head. Return to the sucking.

Unless you're hung like King Kong and they're already lining up around the block to dive into your lap, you've got to *give* head to *get* head. True, there are guys out there who want a man to blow them but don't want to return the favor. I say screw them (or more literally, don't screw them). Reciprocity is a great thing, and you know you want his lips on your cock, so make a good show of it when you're going down on him. Inspire him to try to outdo you. Normally, I don't much care for one-upmanship or competitiveness between partners, but if it raises the temperature in the sack, then by all means, bring the noise!

NO. 33 All Hands on Dick!

By now you may have some good dick-sucking rhythm going, and your lucky playmate is probably lying back and moaning with pleasure. Maybe he's playing with your hair, or squeezing your nipples (points for him if he is), or playing with his own. In the meantime, you've got to get your hands involved. Hold his cock at the base with one hand by making a ring with your index finger and thumb and use a gentle downward pressure. This will keep his dick stiff and upright and in the best position for cock sucking.

If he's extra large, he's probably not accustomed to having anyone take his whole penis anyway, so concentrate on licking and sucking the head and down the sides of the shaft. With one hand, make a tube shape with your fingers and hold it in front of your mouth so that his cock slides through the tube before and after it goes into your mouth. This hand motion will add stimulation to the head and the coronal ridge.

With your mouth around his cock, turn your head clockwise and counterclockwise as you bob up and down. You can move your hands in a gentle twisting motion in the opposite directions as you're twisting your head. To stimulate the underside of his cock, extend your tongue inside your mouth while you're sucking on his willy, and press firmly up on the frenulum while you're sucking. This can create a little more vacuum action too. (Ounce for ounce, your tongue is the strongest muscle in your body, so use it!)

Since the glans is especially sensitive on uncut guys, sliding your tongue or a well-moistened finger (if the foreskin isn't too tight) between the head and foreskin will give him waves of sensation. Some men have sensitive foreskin, so try gently nibbling on the foreskin. Then, flick your tongue over the frenulum and see what he seems to like. If the head of his cock isn't too sensitive, flick your tongue across the glans and urethral opening.

All the while, make sure you're listening to his responses. Some guys like light lips and tongue pressure and light suction. Other guys want you to suck like you're a canister vacuum cleaner. Some guys love to see you slap his dick against your lips, cheeks, or neck. In porn flicks, the guy getting sucked is usually the one slapping his dick on the sucker's face, but if the BJ-giver does it, it's a way to assert that you know what you're doing.

NO. 34! Blow Job Basics

Most dicks curve slightly one way or the other, making certain positions better for oral sex than others. For the purposes of description, I'll describe you, dear reader, as the sucker, and your playmate as the suckee. But feel free to switch positions and roles as your impulses dictate.

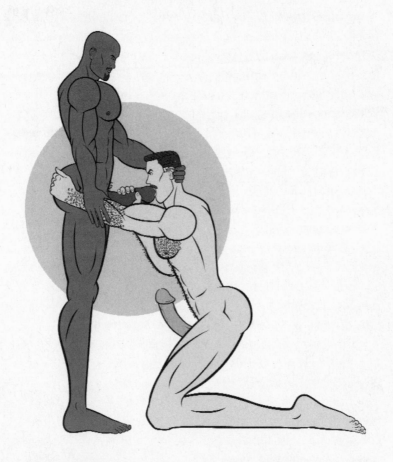

The Classic: If you're not deep-throating yet, then kneeling in front of him while he's standing or sitting is going to be a fine position to give him a good knob-job. Most cocks curve up just slightly, but you'll still be able to get a good portion of his member into your mouth, remembering to use your hands to stroke, fondle, and tickle. **Pros:** From this position you have a lot of control over how deeply into your mouth he penetrates, your hands are free to stimulate other parts of him or yourself, and he can gently or firmly hold your head. This is a great position if you like him to hold your head in place and thrust into your mouth, a technique rather unsubtly called the skull-fuck. **Cons:** If you're a novice and not up to getting skull-fucked quite yet, your gag reflex might be triggered. It's natural for your throat to tense up when it's being invaded, so if you gag, take a little break, relax, and maybe have him sit down to continue (a position that makes it a little harder for him to thrust into you). If it's still a little tricky, try a different position, or have him suck your dick for a while.

Soixante-neuf: Okay, it's the good old sixty-nine position, but it seems more exotic when you say it in French (pronounced: "*swah-san-noof*"). Each of you lies on his side so that his penis is aimed at your mouth and your penis is aimed at his mouth. In this position, you can both suck on each other at the same time. A variation on this idea is a top/bottom position with one guy on his back and the other guy on hands and knees over him. The top/bottom formation is good for novices because the newbie can be on top and control the thrusting into the other guy's mouth, and the guy on bottom can't thrust

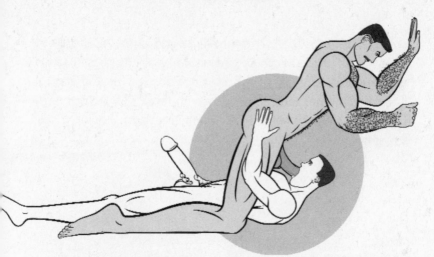

quite as easily. **Pros:** Soixante-neuf is a fantastic feedback loop—the more you're being pleasured, the more you get into sucking him, which pleasures him even more, so he gets more into sucking you. Also, it's great because in English it rhymes with "wine me, dine me." **Cons:** This is sixty-nine! There are no cons.

The Recliner: Lie on your back with your head propped up on some pillows, while he kneels close by so that he can fuck your face. A variation is the modified push-up where you lie flat, no pillows, and he assumes a push-up position with his crotch over your face. From there he can thrust his dick into your mouth. **Pros:** Both positions are totally hot because he gets to thrust at will, and both positions leave your hands free to stimulate yourself or play with the his balls, ass, etc. **Cons:** You aren't in control of the force or depth of his thrusting.

Bed's Edge Face-Fuck: You lie on your back on the bed so that your head dangles backward over the edge. He stands at the edge of the bed behind and above you, sliding his cock into your mouth. Since your head is tilted back, it straightens out your esophagus giving him a straighter passage to slide his dick into. He can put his hands on your body, or he can bend forward and suck your cock at the same time. **Pros:** It's hot to watch and feel the thrusting, and you get to take more of his penis into your mouth. **Cons:** This position can trigger your gag reflex if you're not sufficiently relaxed.

NO. 35 It's All About Sensations

He likes what you're doing because you're confident and you're *way* into the sex. Now, make a good show of it by putting as much of his hard cock in your mouth as you can. You can slowly increase your capacity each time he goes into your mouth. He's too big, you say? Well, congrats, boy—you're the envy of your fellow cocksuckers. Actually, while bigger cocks are often the most visually stimulating, mouths and butts are all shaped and sized differently, so the biggest dick in town may not actually be the one you enjoy chowing down on the most.

If you want to up the ante a little, try adding a new sensation by chomping on an Altoid before oral sex (a technique made popular by Monica Lewinsky, who reportedly employed it before blowing the Commander-in-chief) or rinsing your mouth with minty mouthwash before sucking dick. Cinnamon or mint gum has a similar effect, but remember that mint oils are mild irritants. They may offer a great heating or cooling sensation on his dick, but make sure none of the mouthwash or mint comes in contact with his urethra. It burns.

Another sensation enhancer is ice (you can either suck on an ice cube before you start sucking dick, or you can have an ice cube and his dick in your mouth at the same time). You can alternate between warm and cold sensations by switching between warm tea and cold beverages or ice cubes. Sipping some beer or champagne and then letting it dribble down the shaft of his dick while you're sucking his cock will produce an amazing tingling feeling.

While we're here, let's throw in a couple of don'ts:

Fresh breath is a priority in every intimate activity, but don't brush your teeth just before having oral sex. Brushing your teeth can cause micro cuts in your gums, and for safety's sake, you don't want any open cuts, no matter how small, to come in contact with his precome or spunk.

It's best not to pass out when you're giving head, so remember to breathe through your nose. The great time you're having while kneeling at the altar can cease abruptly, if you turn blue and collapse from lack of oxygen. Resuscitation ain't sexy.

Okay, so "blow job" isn't as accurate a term as "suck job," but we're stuck with the name. But that doesn't mean you shouldn't try blowing on his cock, especially when it's wet with your spit. The cool sensation will send a little chill down his cock. Then put it back into your warm mouth. He'll soon believe you're the sex god you told him you were.

NO. 36 How's It Hanging? The Care and Use of Testicles

Don't forget the twins when you're going down on him. When handled properly, his testicles can produce tons of delicious sensations during sex. Since you've got a pair yourself, you know exactly what it feels like when they're not handled properly—such as when they've been kicked, punched, stomped on, hit with a nine iron, or any of the other wince-producing things done to guys' balls on those wacky home-video TV shows. Those things hurt like a motherfucker. You don't want your playmate yelping in pain unless he specifically tells you, "Make me yelp in pain!"

So give the balls some good attention too. Take a break from going down on him and rest your jaw muscles by gently nibbling on his cojones. But stick to the loose, wrinkly skin surrounding the testicles and epididymis, and don't chomp down on his balls—we don't want you damaging any of the delicate contents. A gentle nibble can feel fantastic, especially if he's hard and his blood is pumping.

In tea-bagging, your man stands above you or straddles you, while he dips his berries into your open mouth. If he's straddling you, move your body until your mouth is directly beneath his nuts. With your fingers, you can form a ring around the base of his ball sac to keep his balls in one nice little bundle. Allow him to dip his balls in and out of your mouth (as one would dip a tea bag in a cup), and use your tongue to give him a nice ball-bath.

Some men like to have their testicles gently tugged, but if you try this, observe his responses very carefully. The best and gentlest way to start—perhaps while his boner is in your mouth—is to encircle his testicles with your index finger and thumb at the top of his tool sac and gently tug them toward you. Make sure you're *tugging,* not *squeezing.* Since many men have sensitive balls, you'll be testing his limits a little bit. If he likes it (moaning, heavy breathing, and/or a little thrashing around will tell the tale), then continue and increase the strength of your tugging very, very, very slowly. Alternate your tugging with rolling his balls around in one open hand.

The ball sac is usually quite wrinkly, and a tongue running across the wrinkles provides some great stimulus, but for different feeling, try tying up your squirrel treats. You can use specially made leather ball-tying straps with snaps, a shoelace, or a long, thin strip of leather. Take the strap and tie it around the scrotum at the top so that it forces your bollocks down and away from your body. This does two things: the sensation of touching or rubbing or licking the balls will be different because the normally wrinkly skin of your ball sac stretches smooth. Also, the feeling of having the balls tied off is similar to their being tugged on by a partner. Ball separators do a similar thing. These little leather contraptions hold your marbles apart so that you can do one thing to one and something else to the other.

NO. 37 Tickle the Taint

For such a small bit of flesh, the perineum (or "taint") is a sensory jackpot. Just south of the testicles and north of the butthole, this miracle inch can be a super sensitive area for some men. Tantric sex practitioners say that stirring up a little excitement in the area can increase blood flow, liberate your latent energy, and release endorphins. At the very least, the endorphins part is on the level, and more endorphins means hotter sex.

Gently stroking the taint or licking lightly can send

waves of delectation to all the right places. As you'll recall, the root of his cock starts there. And the perineum covers the spongy tissues that fill with blood to power his erection—you can sometimes make his erection even stiffer by pressing a couple of fingers there.

The perineum is also sometimes called the "chin rest." If you're facing your fella and performing some fantastic fellatio, and especially if you're sucking on his balls, your chin will be right in the vicinity of his perineum. While you've got his balls in your mouth, press your chin into his perineum and move it from side to side over the root of his cock. Try the same thing with your knuckles by gently pressing on the perineum. You'll be able to feel an extension of the shaft of his cock under the taint. Remember the beginner's BJ technique where you did an impression of an old toothless person? Do that lip trick again and rub your mouth lengthwise along the tube shape—it's like giving an internal blow job. If you go slowly and use enough pressure, this will also stimulate the male G-spot: the prostate gland that lies just beneath. This stimulation can produce mind-blowing orgasms.

NO. 38 Deep-throating— It Ain't Just for Porn Stars

With as much attention as we give to the idea of deep-throating—either learning how to do it, or trying to get our partners to do it to us—you'd think it was the answer to the conflict in the Middle East. Come to think of it, some of those folks probably need a good blow job—it might relax them a little bit. The secrets to deep-throating are simple: practice, patience, and relaxation. If you can learn to overcome your gag reflex—continuing to breathe all the while—then bingo! You're deep-throating.

First, take a look at his cock and notice the direction in which it curves, if it curves at all (most curve up a little bit). For best results while deep-throating, the curve of his member should match the curve of your throat, which curves downward. Do a little geometry here: If his penis curves down, then by kneeling in front of him, you'll be poised for his cock to curve right down your esophagus—perfect! If he curves up, you might try deep-throating from the soixante-neuf position so that he naturally curves down your throat. This is important in sidestepping your gag reflex.

A word about the gag reflex: Just like blinking when you get something in your eye, the gag reflex is a necessary neurological reaction that keeps stuff from getting trapped in your trachea (that tube that carries oxygen from your mouth and nose to your lungs—it's kind of important to keep it clear). It's not something you can entirely train yourself out of doing. If you've ever worn contact lenses, you know that the first 50 times you try to stick the lens in your eye, you blink like mad. Eventually, you train yourself to know when you're deliberately sticking your finger in your eye and you learn to distinguish that activity from the sensations you don't cause yourself. In the same way, you can learn to control the otherwise involuntary gag response whenever you'd like to take a dick down your throat.

Begin by sucking his cock as usual. Next time his

cock hits the back of your throat, try opening your throat in the same way you do when you yawn—it's a widening in the back of the throat. Take him as far down your throat as you can. If you gag, just sit back and give it a minute. He'll appreciate the effort. Keep breathing through your nose and try again when you're relaxed. When you're back at it, if the yawning imagery doesn't quite work, imagine a drink as it goes down the back of your throat. Keeping your throat open is the key.

If you get him all the way down your throat, let him sit there for a moment, or as long as you can. You'll get used to the sensation, and he'll love the feeling of being completely inside your warm mouth. You may notice that the mucous at the back of your throat is a little thicker than saliva—that's normal. Hold his thighs in place to prevent him from thrusting until you're ready. The urge is strong, but you want to make sure your body knows that the monster banging on your tonsils is a welcome intruder.

Once you've become accustomed to the feeling of his dick that far down your throat, you can further astound and impress him by practicing making the muscles in your throat contract—massaging the penis. Try a swallowing motion when he's down your throat. Try sliding his cock into and out of the back of your throat, and soon he'll be singing your praises, if he has the presence of mind to speak at all.

NO. 39

Sweetening Your Spunk

To swallow or not to swallow? That is the question. Well, my friend, that's entirely up to you. Whether your sex is only with a long-term monogamous boyfriend or whether you're tricking with a one-night stand, I encourage you to keep abreast of the medical research in the areas of sexually transmitted diseases. That's your responsibility. My task is to give you helpful hints to give your sex life an added zing.

Some men like the sweet-salty taste of their partners' jism, and some even like the taste of their own. But who wouldn't want his love juice to taste a little bit sweeter? Aside from actual sperm, splooge contains calcium, magnesium, potassium, vitamin B-12, zinc, and fructose to nourish the little sperm. Your spunk had about 15 calories per—ahem—serving. Since your body produces it, the taste of your tapioca toothpaste is affected by your diet and other habits. In fact, some food, like pineapple, melon, strawberries, kiwi, celery, cinnamon, and an all-vegetarian diet, can actually help improve the taste of your semen.

Likewise, a lot of the stuff you ingest can make your cream sauce curdle: Broccoli, high-sodium and salty foods, meat, dairy products, vitamin supplements and many over-the-counter and doctor-prescribed medications all sour the soup. My friend Emil claims he can tell when his boyfriend eats more meat than usual (his boyfriend follows a mostly vegetarian diet), since it made his come taste bitter. Even worse for your bouquet than those foods and pills are coffee (yikes!), cigarettes (damn!), and alcohol (holy crap!).

Add "sweeter spunk" to the list of reason to give up your vices—well, at least *those* vices.

The worst culprit? Let's just say that you shouldn't eat asparagus any night you expect him to be going down on you. You know that nasty smell it imparts to your piss? It does the same to your spunk.

If you hate the taste or texture of his home brew, you may want to practice deep-throating (see Secret #38). If he's far enough down your throat when he shoots, you'll never taste a thing—plus he might put you in his will for making his knees turn to jelly.

NO. 40 You Want Me to Do What? Rimming and Enjoying It!

Rimming is one of those practices that as a concept usually stops newbies dead in their tracks. Licking someone's asshole sounds like something you'd have to do if you lost a bet. It ain't. It's a damn fine thing, so people should dig in and enjoy. That's not to say some people just aren't interested—but converts will tell you that, like so many things sexual, the idea first repulsed them but then they saw the light.

Your tushie has tons of those little nerve endings we love so much. To ignore all those little pleasure pods is simply inexcusable. Stimulating these nerves also causes involuntary anal sphincter contractions, which can add to your pleasure.

Of course, the first priority in a good rim job (also called anilingus) is a spotless bum. When you're showering, slide a soapy finger up your chocolate starfish and make sure you're nice and clean. Since soap can be an anal irritant (and it tastes nasty), make sure you rinse everything well with water before getting down to business.

Perhaps you've never rimmed before, but you realize your partner is giving you hints that he wants you to rim him (he might put his legs in the air, arch his back, and prod you to go lower when you're sucking his dick, for example). You might then start teasing the outer parts of his butt, scrotum, or perineum with your tongue until you feel comfortable enough to move toward his anus. There's nothing wrong with telling him it's your first time rimming someone. He'll probably help you through it.

If you're the one being rimmed, you can lie facedown on your stomach or on your back with heels in the air, or you can stand and bend over the edge of a chair or bed. You can spread your cheeks for better access, or you can let him spread them for you. Rimming is also fantastic in the soixante-neuf position because it necessitates a lot of body contact (though usually only one man can rim at a time in this position).

If you're the rimmer, it's best to start with some kissing and licking on the outer rump and move gradually toward home plate. The deeper you push your tongue, the better it feels. Again, lubrication is key, so make sure you use plenty of saliva or some store-bought lube. A great approach is to alternate soft licks and stiff-tongued probing with a little gentle nibbling and even humming. Humming? When your face is pretty well buried in his ass, try moaning or humming. The vibrations produced are quite unusual—it might be a new experience for your playmate.

If you're the rimmer, you'll probably have to decide when the rimming is done. Anyone who says he's had enough of you tonguing his asshole is lying.

CHAPTER 5

Doing the Butt—a Primer

★★★★★★★★★★★★★★★★★★★★★★★★★★★★★★★★★★★★★★

NO. 41 Screw Him and Screw Your Preconceptions at the Same Time

For the sake of discussion, let's chat about the terms "top" and "bottom"—what they mean to anal sex and where the terms can lead us astray. When we're talking about butt-fucking, the top is the man who is the penetrator (whether he's using his dick, a dildo, a strap-on, a cucumber, a finger, etc.) and the bottom is the man who is being penetrated. It sounds simple, even if you switch roles with your partner over the course of a rendezvous or a relationship. (The terms more commonly used in the recent past were "Greek-Active," meaning "top," and

"Greek-Passive," meaning "bottom." (Apparently, ancient Greek men liked to fuck each other a lot.) I'd argue that those terms are misnomers because anyone who's been with a bossy bottom—and you know if you have—knows that the "Greek-Passive" man who just gave you the sweaty aerobic sex workout of your life was anything but passive.

"Top" and "bottom" mean different things in BDSM (bondage/discipline/sado-masochism) play than they do here. In BDSM play, the top is the one who is in control of the scene, and the bottom is the submissive person. (Nominally, at least—I know of at least one bottom who totally controls the scene through subtle manipulation, even when the top is ordering him around.) The terms can lead us astray when we get hung up on roles that we assume correspond to our sexual preferences. Most gay men who in engage in anal sex—and not all gay men like butt love, by the way—are neither total tops nor total bottoms, but exist somewhere on a scale between the two extremes. Some guys prefer to fuck but will take it up the ass on occasion, and some guys love to get fucked but will be tops when the mood strikes. And many men will take it up the wazoo as well as be the top—and like both acts equally. Big deal, you say? Well, it can be a big deal, if we buy into the stereotypes that go along with topping and bottoming.

The stereotype is that men who are tops are more butch or hung or aggressive while men who are bottoms are less well-hung, feminine, or passive. It's high time to discard that crap—especially the notion that you can look at or talk to someone and tell whether he's a top or bottom. Those clichés are simply barriers to good sex. If you're a butch cigar-chomping daddy and like it best when you're getting pounded with your heels in the air, so be it. You can still be masculine, and you can still kiss! And if you're a mincing queen, but you like to stick your dick into a sweet ass, by God, you should fuck away! By the same token, if you don't enjoy taking it up the ass, then that's ok too. Don't be pressured into doing something sexually that you don't enjoy simply because you think it's expected of you or your "type." Don't let preconceived notions about *who* should do *what* to *whom* get in the way of exploring your sexual tastes and enjoying yourself.

NO. 42 Know Your Ass Anatomy

The butt is a fascinating and complex place, so if you want to engage in butt play, you'd better be working with the upstairs head as well as the downstairs one. Anyone who plans to fuck or get fucked really ought to know what's going on inside those luscious flesh globes known as the booty (note: "booty" is not a medically recognized technical term).

Anal sex involves a lot of parts, but for this discussion, let's explore the anus, the rectum, and the colon. The whole shebang is the body's way of getting rid of waste. Waste passes from the colon (the end of the digestive tract) into the roughly eight-inch-long chamber called the rectum, then out of the body through the anus.

The anus has two bands of circular muscles: the internal and external sphincters. The external sphincter is controlled voluntarily by the central nervous system, the same system that allows you to voluntarily walk and talk and pick your nose. Most of the time, the external sphincter muscle is under your control: When you've got to take a dump but you're still a few minutes away from a bathroom, you can keep your external sphincter clenched until you can get to the facilities. The internal sphincter is not usually under your conscious control. It's regulated by the autonomic nervous system, which also keeps your blood pumping and keeps you breathing when you're asleep, or unconscious, or passed out from a night of too many margaritas.

Here's how it all works together: Waste remains in the colon until your body is ready to eliminate it. When the colon moves waste along, your rectal reflex is automatically triggered. The internal sphincter relaxes (it widens), and when you're ready to voluntarily relax your external sphincter, you can make a deposit at the porcelain bank. Most of the time the rectum is empty after a bowel movement, except for some residual traces of waste. But, beware that butt sex is never a 100 percent clean operation, so the first thing anyone can do to enjoy anal sex is to understand that simple biological fact. An asshole is an asshole is an asshole, and it will never be a silk purse. Don't expect it to be. Anal sex can still be a hell of a lot of fun. I promise.

NO. 43 Spring Cleaning for Bottoms— Prepping for Butt Play

Anal sex can be an enormously pleasurable sex act, but getting hung up on whether you're clean enough can put a damper on your ability to enjoy it. No one likes an unplanned mess—our "ick" response is human nature. And there's no getting around the fact that we all have to drop the kids off at the pool on a more or less daily basis. Still, with some proper attention to diet and cleanliness, you shouldn't have any trouble surfing where the sun don't shine. And with a good attitude about the inevitable occasional accident, you can deal with the unexpected and still have a gay ol' time.

So plan ahead. It's takes about 24 hours for food to go from your gullet to your gazoo, so if you know ahead of time that you're going to be "hosting," then consider eating lightly the day before. Dairy, meat, and processed foods tend to gum up your internal works, so slow down on the cheeseburgers. Instead, eat more fiber. Most Americans only get half the recommended amount of dietary fiber. Fiber is the part of many foods (fresh fruits and veggies, legumes, whole grains, nuts) that your body cannot digest. As the fiber moves through your digestive tract, it drags all kinds of gunk with it, keeping your intestines and colon so clean you could eat off 'em—figuratively speaking. A high-fiber diet can prevent diarrhea and constipation, and it keeps your potty visits regular and your stool firm—and that means less toilet paper and less presex cleanup. Eating fiber is good for butt sex and it's just a generally healthy thing to do.

Having a bowel movement fairly soon (up to a few hours) before anal sex can help you feel cleaner and lighter. Then jump in the shower, stick a soapy finger up your butt and make sure to rinse out any irritating soap. Swab, rinse, and repeat as needed. That's often all the prep work you need to do.

Some men prefer to use an enema or douche prior to sex. That's fine too, but rather than use the solution in ready-made kits like Fleet, you could buy an empty refillable enema kit or empty the solution from a ready-made package and refill the container with regular lukewarm tap water. The solution in those ready-made enemas is designed to break up constipation blockages with chemicals that will likely do more work on your insides than you want them to. Your rectal tissues are very absorbent and somewhat sensitive, so you don't want to irritate them unnecessarily. Douching occasionally is fine, but if you use douches too frequently your body can become dependent on them, and you may eventually require an enema every time you need to have a poo.

NO. 44 For Tops: Preparing Your Partner Through Relaxation

To prevent pain and injury, you—as the top—need to make sure that your partner is fully prepared for anal sex. Some guys are ready to bend over and be penetrated at the drop of a hat (or the drop of your trousers), but plenty of men need a bit of mental and physical preparation before taking it up the ass—even if they're dying to get fucked.

Even if you're strictly a top, there are plenty of reasons why you should examine your own tush regularly. By slipping a finger into your ass for a minute or two each time you shower and by massaging your prostate and feeling your sphincter muscles tense and relax, you'll not only learn how these parts work (useful info when it comes to sex with bottoms), but you'll also be improving your health. A relaxed sphincter can lessen your chances of having chronic constipation, and a routinely massaged prostate gland might reduce your chances of getting prostate cancer.

Back to the sex. The anus is primarily an exit rather than an entrance. Before entering his velvety nether regions, you have to know his hole really wants you and that it's really ready for you. In other words, you have to warm up the butthole. Massaging his ass cheeks, rimming, and circling the tootsie tip with a lubed finger are all good ways to start making friends with his hole. What you cannot do is start banging away like an amateur at the entrance to his booty.

To prepare to go dirt-roading, you'll need to start by relaxing his anal canal, the inch-long space between the sphincters. Using that lubed finger, play with the pucker of his hole by rubbing in a circular motion. His anus, like his genitals and nipples, gets a rush of blood when he's aroused, so your gentle circular motion will definitely rev his engine. When you can feel his sphincter relaxing, you might try inserting that lubed finger (hands must be clean, fingernails must be trimmed!) up to your first knuckle. Pause. Let him feel your digit inside him and wait until you can feel his ass relax again before you move any farther inside. Proceed when you get the proverbial thumbs-up to sticking your finger up his ass

Depending on your partner's mood, he may be receptive to you trying the same thing with two fingers or three. Go slow, communicate with him about what you're doing and how he's feeling, and ask whether he wants more or wants you to go slower. It's usually best if you don't stroke his dick—not just yet anyway. Let him concentrate on relaxing, rather than concentrating on his hard-on.

Once your finger is inside, aim toward his navel rather than his tailbone. By heading in that direction you can locate his prostate gland, the male G-spot that lies about three inches inside his lower rectal cavity. It's the size of a walnut and feels a bit like the muscle pad at the base of your thumb. The more aroused he is, the easier it will be to find. Insert your index finger and stroke it with a gentle "come here" finger motion. (Doing this during a blow job can result in an explosive orgasm. As a little warm-up prior to fucking, it will have him salivating for more butt play.)

NO. 45 For Bottoms: Get Into the Groove

Uneasiness about sex and performance anxiety can be part of a self-fulfilling prophecy: They'll make your sphincters tense up, and tense sphincters mean painful butt burgling. One essential element to an enjoyable first time (or an enjoyable 1,001st time, for that matter) is a relaxed set o' sphincters. Plenty of people think that anal sex has to be painful the first time or the first several times you do it, but that's a myth. There is no reason it ever has to hurt if you take your time, communicate with your partner, and relax. To ease into penetration, try a few of these relaxation techniques:

★ Have your partner enter you very slowly while you take long, deep, cleansing breaths. On each out-breath, imagine all the tension running out of your shoulders, arms, legs, and back. Once he's all the way inside you, rest there for a minute to get accustomed to the feeling of fullness (it may feel like you have to go to the bathroom, and the sensation can be disconcerting to newbies).

★ As he's entering you, bear down. Make a silent grunt—you'll see it's the same muscle movement you use when you're trying to poop. It might feel counter-intuitive—as though you're trying to push his penis out of you—but grunting or bearing down actually works to relax the muscles in the pelvic region.

★ If you're especially tense, try having an orgasm before you let your partner attempt penetration. Any reason to come is a good one, right? Well, aside from the warm and fuzzy afterglow, having an orgasm will relax your whole body, and a relaxed body can get fucked more easily.

★ Make sure you don't stroke your baloney pony until his tool is all the way inside. Your arousal tenses up your anus. It will feel great once he's inside, but in the meantime, jerking off is like slamming that little puckered door shut.

★ Guide him in! Use your hands. He may be experienced at this, but even if he is, all asses are different, so be prepared to play ground-traffic control.

★ While you're sucking each other's cocks or making out, insert a butt plug in your ass and leave it there for a while (it's what the porn stars sometimes do before anal sex on camera). Aside from feeling nice, it helps you relax with the sensation of having something roughly cock-shaped up your ass. When you're ready to fuck, pull the plug out and replace it with his meat rocket.

★ Experienced bottoms often like to take the penis in all at once and then relax around it. A squatting approach and a lot of deep breaths help here: deep breath in, then slide the cock in on the exhale. Pause and relax.

No. 46 For Tops: What to Do Once You're Inside

Okay, boys, the bottom guy is nice and relaxed and he's probably enjoyed what you've been doing to his ass. You are hard and ready to play hide the sausage. So whip it out! Lightly lube your dick and roll on a condom, making sure to not to use any with nonoxynol-9 (see condom section below). Slap some water-based lube on the outside of the condom and lube your partner's anus. Don't be afraid to use a couple of fingers to get some lube inside past the sphincters.

Press the head of your cock against the backdoor to announce the delivery of your package. If you've properly made friends with his ass, his hole will probably respond with a few contractions. With your hand on your penis (and maybe his hands helping you too), guide it slowly toward the promised land. Enter the butt, aiming toward the navel until you're past the internal sphincter. At this point you'll probably be able to feel a few of those lovely sphincter contractions.

The rectum is an S-shaped tube with two curves along its length. Just inside the anal opening, the rectum goes up toward your navel, then curves and angles up the other way, toward your back. After your cock head is in past the sphincters, aim for the tailbone to avoid hitting the first curve. Insertion at the wrong angle or ramming into the rectum walls can cause pain and discomfort. If you go slowly, and take as much time as the bottom guy wants, he'll stay aroused but relaxed.

The net result of the bottom guy's being relaxed is that he will enjoy it more and he will be able to go for a longer session. If you rush this part of butt play, he might feel uncomfortable or become tense, which can cause injury— and nobody wants a sprained sphincter.

We'll get to the various positions in a little bit, but here's something to think about while you're making sure he's relaxed: He's not just a hole, he's got a whole body to play with. Gentle kisses, nibbles, caresses, and nipple tweaks all feel good, and they'll keep him in the amorous mood while he's relaxing onto your cock.

NO. 47 Condoms!

Using condoms will reduce the likelihood of transmitting some STDs, including HIV. That's an indisputable medical fact, despite what conspiracy theorists will tell you. There is absolutely no harm in wearing a condom, and studies have demonstrated (over and over and over again) that proper use of rubbers reduces the transmission of many sexually transmitted diseases. For a complete listing of STDs, means of transmission, and disease prevention, go to www.gayhealthchannel.com.

While condoms don't protect against all diseases (some STDs like HPV and herpes can be transmitted through skin-to-skin contact), consistent and correct condom use can reduce the risk of HIV transmission by up to 10,000 times. Condoms are available almost everywhere and are inexpensive (less than a dollar for one). They're disposable, and they come in a variety of flavors, textures, shapes, sized, and colors.

If you're going to fuck—ever—you should always have a supply of condoms on hand, and you need to know how to put one on. If you're uncut, pull the foreskin back. Unwrap the condom, figure out which direction it unrolls, pinch the reservoir tip between two fingers of one hand (or if there isn't a reservoir, pinch the air out of the half-inch at the tip of the condom), and roll it down over your erect dick. Putting a few drops of water-based or silicone-based lube on the inside will increase the top guy's pleasure, and generously lubing the outside of the condom once it's on will increase the bottom's pleasure. Air in the condom, lack of lube, or a too-tight condom can increase the chances of condom breakage, so pay attention when you're putting it on. If you like to play rough, you might want to try some thicker condoms that are specially designed for rougher play.

Speaking of being thicker and tighter, there are a number of different kinds of condoms to choose from, depending on your endowment and on their intended use. Stay away from anything you can get from a bathroom vending machine—unless, of course, that's all you can get your hands on and you're going to fuck in the bathroom stall one way or the other. Better you should use a crummy rubber than not use one at all. But for those times when you've planned ahead, select a brand that fits well and feels good. Homos, like Boy Scouts, should be well-prepared.

Most condoms are made from latex: a strong, thin type

of rubber—hence the nickname "rubbers." Latex condoms are inexpensive, very thin, and protect against HIV by trapping the love juice inside during the fucking or sucking. They're compatible with water-based lube (not "water-soluble") and silicone lube, but oil-based lubes and oily food products will break down latex.

Natural condoms, often called lambskin condoms, are not useful in the prevention of HIV transmission. The pores in lambskin condoms are larger than the HIV virus, which means the virus can pass through them. Since neither of you is worried about pregnancy, don't mess with natural condoms. For men who are allergic to latex, there are polyurethane condoms. A miracle of modern technology, they are thinner than latex, almost invisible when worn, hypoallergenic, and taste- and odor-free. But they're a bit less elastic than latex, so finding the right size is important. These space-age polyurethane jimmy hats are compatible with all lubes (including oil-based).

Condoms come lubed, nonlubed, or lubed with a spermicide. Stay away from the spermicidal condoms. Nonoxynol-9, the spermicide most often used on condoms, has been shown to kill HIV in the test tube, but it can do more harm than good because it can irritate the rectal lining, making the bottom guy more likely to absorb the virus. Prelubed condoms (without spermicide) sound as convenient as a KFC spork— "It's a spoon and it's a fork!" But you have to read the package carefully to know if they're right for you. The whole lubed-or-not-lubed ordeal can be complicated if you're using silicone toys. That wacky silicone paradox (silicone lube will destroy silicone toys) applies here. You should always stick to non-lubed condoms (and supply your own water-based lube) or use prelubed with water-based lube only.

Whether you're hung like Mr. Ed or Jiminy Cricket, you can find just the right love glove to maximize pleasure and ensure a good fit. Large condoms are labeled clear as day. And it can't hurt one's ego marching up to the cash register at the Quik-E-Mart with a box of supersize rubbers in hand.

The marketing geniuses at the condom companies also know that no one is going to march up to the counter and proudly slap down a box of condoms labeled "small," so if you need a tighter-fitting condom, look for key words on the package like "snug" and "fit." You definitely want it to fit right. Too snug, and it might break (as well as strangle all the sensation out of your dick). Too loose, and it might slip off, or even just slide down too far, exposing more skin and making you more susceptible to the skin-to-skin communicable STDs. There are many combinations of shapes and sizes, including some with a looser "balloon top" or oversize tip. With the aid of a few drops of lube, an oversize tip can provide just the right kind of friction.

If you've always used one brand and you're just now exploring other options in the wide world of condoms, go to ye olde sex shoppe or condom specialty store (or online) and buy a few varieties. Once you've rolled a flavored condom onto a hard dick, a willing partner could help you conduct a taste-testing experiment—in the name of science, naturally. Try a few different brands and styles when you're having anal sex. When you switch positions, switch condom brands. To determine the perfect condom for each of you, both the bottom and top can rate the condoms for texture, smell, sensitivity, and elasticity.

No. 48

Anal Etiquette

Far be it from me to suggest that your hot bone-burying session should in any way be influenced by Emily Post. Still, there are a few heretofore-unwritten etiquette lessons that—if you learn and heed them—will totally impress your partner. Being known as a *considerate* fuck will only add to your burgeoning rep as a *superhot* fuck. Think of this as bum-love charm school.

Bum Love Charm Lesson One: The top should only poke butt as long as the bottom wants to. Granted, some guy's poop chutes are made of steel and can take an "ape throwing American Tourister luggage"-style beating for hours at a time without getting worn out. Not everyone has such an ironclad ass. Even the most relaxed, lubed, well-prepared bottom can endure the accumulated effects of rectal punishment for only so long. You don't want to cause injury to his rump, or ruin the mood by fucking for longer then you're welcome.

Bum Love Charm Lesson Two: In addition to setting a reasonable time frame, the bottom is in charge of how much lube is used and how deeply he gets fucked.

Bum Love Charm Lesson Three: Before you wear each other out, make sure to mix it up! Don't be afraid to try several positions. Whether you're the top or the bottom or both, suggest switching positions. Even a slight alteration in angle or rhythm can let one or both of you rest from a physically taxing position. This is also a good way to make sure that one guy isn't doing all the heavy lifting.

Bum Love Charm Lesson Three Corollary: If it

feels good and you're both loving it, don't interrupt your flow just to switch positions. There's no standard time frame for any given position, and there's no East German judge knocking off points for a lopsided dismount.)

Bum Love Charm Lesson Four: Even in the throes of passion, the message can be confused by its delivery, so be careful when you're barking instructions. Yelling, "Do me faster, do me deeper!" can sound like, "This is great sex—I'm loving this!" Or it can come off like, "You idiot, don't you know how to fuck?" Practice barking out your demands so they don't sound like insults. A simple "Oh, yes!" before the "Do me faster!" will boost his ego and keep you both in the moment.

Bum Love Charm Lesson Five: Tops should try both short and long strokes, for the sake of variety and also because some guys prefer one kind to the other when they're getting fucked. Long, slow strokes can produce a lot of good friction in the anal canal, and shorter strokes can be great for stimulating the prostate. Some tops like the feeling of sliding all the way out before taking a plunge all the way back in. While the feeling can be phenomenal, it can also trap air inside the bottom's bottom—and that can be painful. Unsure what he prefers? Just ask.

Bum Love Charm Lesson Six: For safety's sake, don't suck any body parts that have been up anyone's ass. Also, don't touch any body parts with toys or fingers if those toys or fingers have been up anyone's butt. If you're coordinated enough, keep one hand for dick stroking (both your dick and his—use the right hand if you're right-handed) and the other hand (your left one, smarty-pants) for ass play. If you put your fingers in your own ass, wash your hands with antibacterial soap before playing with his ass.

★ 108 ★

NO. 49

Delayed Gratification

A hot, sweaty, butt-loving session could push almost anyone toward orgasmic inevitability faster than a cashmere sweater sale at Barney's. Since there's no getting around the refractory period (that downtime between an orgasm and your ability to get another erection), you don't want to blow your wad too quickly, or at least not until he catches up with you. Having a partner who finishes just as you're starting to get warmed up can be extremely disappointing as well. Here are some tricks of the trade (or should they be called trade tricks? Or tricks for tricks?) that can help you keep going longer than Bob Dole on Viagra. Sorry, bad example.

The term "premature ejaculation" is often used to mean one partner having an orgasm before both partners are satisfied. That's a rather subjective definition, especially if we're talking about a top guy fucking one of those ironclad bottom guys for whom "satisfaction" requires almost superhuman acts of penetration over the course of several hours. True premature ejaculation is a condition characterized by the inability to control ejaculation in the first few moments of sex—usually just after penetration. It usually happens to guys who are relatively new to sex, but it can happen occasionally (just like occasional impotence) to almost anyone at any time. We're men, not machines, damn it!

The causes of chronic premature ejaculation can be physical or psychological, so talk to a doctor if you've tried a few at-home techniques without success. The techniques we'll discuss here are not a replacement for psychological therapy or a medical diagnosis, but they will help some guys keep it stiff a little bit longer.

Learning to identify your sexual response is perhaps the easiest way to delay orgasm. Secret #18 discusses strengthening your PC muscles to delay orgasm, making your hardons harder, and to learning to identify ejaculatory inevitability through masturbation. Once you know you're about to get to the point of no return, try one of these techniques on yourself.

Deep breathing can relax your whole body and lessen some of the built-up sexual tension that can push you to ejaculatory inevitability. When you get close to coming, have your partner stop whatever pleasurable thing he's doing and take several deep, cleansing breaths. You can send the soldier back into battle once you've relaxed a bit.

Alternatively, you can try the squeeze technique. Grip just under the head of the penis with your thumb and forefinger when you can feel the spasms of orgasm coming on. Squeeze firmly until the feeling of ejaculatory inevitability passes. The same squeezing technique can be applied to the base of the shaft of the penis.

If your partner's breathing quickens and he lets you know that he's getting close to orgasm, you can try the testicle tug on him. That's when you make a ring around the top of his ball sac with your thumb and forefinger and gently pull his balls down away from his body. One of the natural physiological components of an approaching orgasm is for the balls to contract toward the body cavity. By pulling them down and away, you're tricking his body into thinking it isn't time yet. Most guys last longer the second time, so if either of you shoots early, relax for a few minutes then go for it again!

NO. 50

Finishing Touches

Pulling it out properly is almost as important as putting it in properly. Some guys get a little nauseous after getting fucked, usually from having anal sex while they're too tense. The nausea can be exacerbated if the top pulls out too quickly. A hasty exit can cause the muscles in the anus to spasm—and not in a good, orgasmic kind of way. Even if he's telling you, "Get out of my ass right now!" you should slide out slowly.

My own recent informal poll suggests that the pornos are right on this account: We love to see the money shot. Watching the splooge burst out of a throbbing dick is totally hot, so if you're doing the fucking, be sure to take advantage of our penchant for visual stimulation by putting on a little show: Pull out, discretely (and quickly) remove the condom, and stroke yourself to a happy ending. A visible sperm geyser is almost like a pat on the back for a job well-done—for both partners. Shoot on his chest, on his neck, on his face, on his ass cheeks, or anywhere else he likes. Just keeping your home brew away from any broken skin and from all his orifices, including his urethra. Neither of you should use the other's spunk as jerk-off lube. It's the top's job to scoop up the used condoms and dispose of them somewhere discreet, like a covered trash can where his cat can't snatch them up and use them as chew toys.

Your host (or you, if you hosted) should have plenty of towels handy (remember that dark towels minimize the "ick" factor) to wipe up the love juice, sweat, marshmallow paste, honey, and any other residual mess. If one or both of you has to run to the bathroom, it's cool to do so. You have about a three- to four-minute window of opportunity to catch your breath, wipe off the splooge, wash your hands, and return to the scene of the crime for some postcoital cuddling if you are with a lover or date-date, or to bring a warm, wet towel if you're playing with a casual trick.

After you've cuddled a bit, you should clean up more thoroughly. Any body parts that came in contact with the anal region should be thoroughly washed with antibacterial soap. If you can, you should also take a piss afterward; it helps clear the urethra of the kinds of cooties that can cause urethritis ("It burns when I pee"). A shared shower can be a fantastic postsex activity. Gentle kissing and gently scrubbing each other's bodies with a soapy loofah or shower mitt will keep the all-over tingles continuing throughout the afterglow. Take a look at Secret #63 for the proper cleaning of your sex toys.

Feeling a little sore after an active anal sesh? Well, a little tenderness is to be expected. In fact, some men love having a gentle reminder of a good reaming for the next day—every time they sit down. A little good pain (like sore muscles after a workout) is fine. Too much pain (like watching *Highway to Heaven* reruns on PAX TV)? Well, either you didn't read this chapter thoroughly, or you were a little too rough, or you decided to have at it without enough lube. Make a mental note not to do that again. If you're having bad pain, or pain doesn't go away within a few days, or if you notice any blood—especially if bleeding persists—see a doctor.

CHAPTER 6

Pole Positions

★★★

NO. 51

High Heels Position

There are literally hundreds of variations on sexual positions—thousands if you add a third or fourth person to the equation. The next few sections describe two-person positions, along with the benefits for each partner (with examples provided by our esteemed panel of homos). You should try a few different positions with a new partner until you find one or two or 15 that you like. Then you should try them all again! Factors like height, weight, the shape of cocks and rectums, mood, and flexibility will affect whether you're able to fuck while standing, sitting, or hanging from a chandelier. Initially, the bottom guy should determine which position you start in, since he's the one who's most likely to feel discomfort if you're not in a good position.

Bill and Antonio's favorite position is the **High Heels** position, Bill (usually a bottom) lies on his back with his legs spread or with his knees tucked to his chest. Antonio lies on top of him if Bill's legs are down, or he kneels in front of Bill and holds his ankles up. Bill can also put his feet on Antonio's chest or throw his legs over Tony's shoulders.

Benefits for the top: "I can go deep in this position," says Antonio. "I love watching my dick go into Bill's ass. Sometimes he likes me to go as deep as I can, and this angle allows me to thrust all the way in." This position works especially well for partners of varying height.

Benefits for the bottom: "This position is great for eye contact," says Bill. "Antonio can fuck me really deeply this way—plus, I can pull him down to me and kiss him while he's inside me." It's also a great position for a lazy bottom—not that Bill is a lazy bottom.

Extra Credit: To get the best access to Bill's ass so he can go deep, Antonio puts a pillow or cushion covered with a towel under Bill's tush. Billy likes his toes sucked, and when his legs are up, Antonio can easily get them into his mouth.

NO. 52 Ride 'Em, Cowboy Position

In this position, Keith is the bottom, but he squats over Toby, the top, who lies flat on his back. **Ride 'Em, Cowboy** works well with the "all at once" insertion technique. Keith can start on his knees or on his feet and he can aim Toby's dick at his hole. Keith can slide all the way down Toby's dick and sit in that position to relax. Once Toby is all the way in, he can thrust upward, but Keith still has control over how deeply Toby fucks him. Keith has to make sure not to clench his butt cheeks too hard when he moves himself into a new position—it's easy to tense up that way.

Benefits for the top: "I love watching Keith take my dick and fuck himself on it. I can play with his dick or pinch my nipples and just watch."

Benefits for the bottom: "I can't always take Toby's dick all at once. If I need a little more time, I'm in control of how deep he goes, and I can set the rhythm."

Extra Credit: When Keith is totally relaxed and enjoying getting fucked, he can put his feet on the ground near Toby's armpits and lean back, supporting himself on his hands near Toby's feet. From this angle, Toby can thrust upward more easily.

NO. 53

Reverse Missionary Position

Paul lies facedown on his stomach, and Marco lies on top of him, facing the same way, and inserting him from behind. In this position, Marco has total control of the depth and frequency of his thrusting. The **Reverse Missionary** works well for these two because Paul occasionally likes to come without touching himself and Marco likes to feel his chest and stomach on Paul's back. This position allows for a slightly shallower penetra-

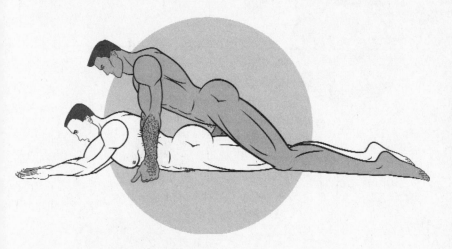

tion than other positions.

Benefits for the top: "It's great to have total control over how hard I fuck Paul. It's a great end to a role-play game where I'm in charge. I can nibble his earlobes and talk dirty to him while he's virtually pinned down by my weight."

Benefits for the bottom: "This is a great position for when

I'm in a 'take me now, do with me what you will' mood, especially since it's hard for me to stroke my dick when he's fucking me in this position. I can't always do it, but this is one position that lets me shoot without touching myself. It's erotic because I'm not in control—I can feel his weight on me, and I can feel and hear his heavy breathing while he's just enjoying my ass."

Extra credit points: By putting down a cushion covered by a towel under Paul's hips (in case he shoots while he's getting fucked), it raises his ass up just enough so that Marco can thrust more easily.

NO. 54

Doggie-Style Position

Okay, so it's not exactly a s e c r e t . **Doggie-style** is a classic, and it's a favorite for T.S. and Dennis. Dennis gets on his hands

and knees and T.S. kneels behind him. T.S. can hold Dennis's hips or shoulders and pull him onto his dick. It's a good angle for T.S. to directly stimulate Dennis's prostate gland, plus if the mood strikes them, T.S. can give Dennis's ass a nice, loud smack. With his legs at a 90-degree angle to his back, Dennis's anal passage and rectum straighten, which makes deep thrusting more comfortable. The position can be difficult for beginner bottoms because of how deep the top is able to thrust.

Benefits for the top: "I really get off watching my dick go into Dennis's butt. Plus, it's doggie-style! Who doesn't love that?" It's also a good position for deep penetration.

Benefits for the bottom: "It feels comfortable because of the angle, plus I can support myself with one arm and stroke myself with the other hand. I like feeling his balls slap against my ass cheeks."

Extra credit: Try this with the bottom guy bent forward over a table or the back of a sofa.

NO. 55 Ostrich Position

This position is a variation on the kneeling Doggie-style position, but with the bottom bending forward and resting his head on a pillow, just as an ostrich buries its head in the sand. The **Ostrich** is good for Peter and Jim when Jim is on top because he's 5 foot 10 to Peter's 6 foot 4—a difference of half a foot. Peter gets into position with his knees spread a little farther apart to adjust the angle for Jim's shorter legs.

Benefit for the top: "It's a great position because I like to

be able to jerk Peter off while I'm fucking him. I love hearing his muffled grunts into the pillow, and I like how he can use both hands to spread his ass for me."

Benefits for the bottom: "I can bury my face and moan and groan as loudly as I like because the sound gets muffled—somewhat. The noise really turns Jim on, and he fucks me harder when he hears me moaning."

Extra credit: If they really get into it, Jim can get off his knees and enter Peter from the same angle while standing with his knees bent, sumo wrestler-style. From that angle, Jim can thrust more quickly.

NO. 56 Scissors Position

Scott and Sam like the **Scissors** position. It's slightly more complicated than most positions, but both guys like the intimacy of this configuration. They lie on their

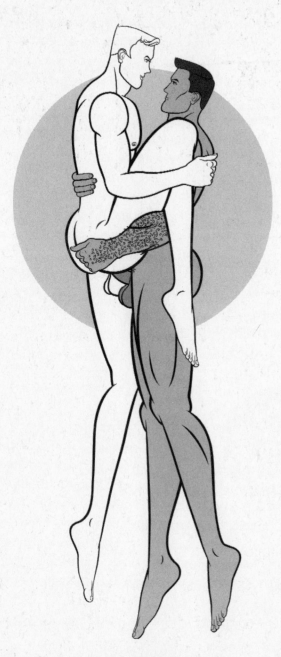

sides, facing each other. Sam pulls one knee up toward his chest (since he's on his side, it's his upper leg, or the leg he's not resting on). This gives Scott's mast access to Sam's porthole. Scott can hold up Sam's knee to vary the angle of entry.

Benefits for the top: "I get to look into Sam's face when we're having sex. We can hold each other and there's a lot of body contact. It's really intimate and I can kiss him and suck on his neck and stuff."

Benefits for the bottom: "When we're facing each other, I can control how deep Scott goes. If I need him to not go so deep, I can pull my legs together a little bit."

Extra credit: From this position, the two can roll over so that Scott is on his back in the **Ride 'Em, Cowboy** position—all without ever having to pull out. Also, they can roll so that Sam is on his back in the **High Heels** position, again without Scott having to pull out.

NO. 57 La-Z-Boy Position

This sitting position is like the **Ride 'Em, Cowboy,** except that the bottom and top are both facing the same direction. Andy and Steve coined the name **La-Z-Boy** because Steve sits back in a roomy chair or on the couch and Andy squats over him or sits on his lap as though he's settling into a recliner. This is another position that allows the bottom to control of how deep and frequent the top drives into him.

Benefits for the top: "I get to watch Andy go to town on

my cock. I can hold his hips and pull him down onto my lap. And I love the feel of his ass all over the front of my hips and thighs."

Benefits for the bottom: "I can really fuck myself as hard as I like on Steve's dick because it's right there pointing up at me. Sometimes he wraps his arms around my torso and just hangs on, thrusting just a little bit. It's a great G-spot position."

Extra points: "I can lean back and support myself a foot or so higher by putting both hands behind me on the top edge of the couch," says Andy. "That way Steve can thrust into me from below."

NO. 58

Thumper Position

Also called the "spoons" position, this is when both lovers lie on their sides, facing the same direction. This angle allows for shallow penetration, and since the top can't thrust as easily, the rhythm is slower and gentler. Christopher and Todd like this position because both of them were primarily tops with other lovers, and they wanted to practice versatility with each other by using a less advanced

position. Christopher calls it the **Thumper** because the quick short movements that Todd makes remind him of Thumper's leg thumping from *Bambi*.

Benefits for the top: "It's a good position to help us both ease into being bottoms for each other. I can reach around and play with Christopher's nipples or his dick."

Benefits for the bottom: "It doesn't hit my prostate directly this way, and I prefer that."

Extra credit: If you're having condomless sex (recommended only for monogamous couples who've been tested for STDs), you can both fall asleep while the top is still inside his partner.

NO. 59

Log-Splitter Position

The **Log-Splitter** is a variation of the **High Heels** position, with the bottom guy lying on his side. Brent lies on his side while Dan stands upright behind him, usually at the edge of the bed, perpendicular to Brent's body. Dan can fuck Brent deeply or less so, depending on whether Brent opens his legs wide or keeps them together.

Benefit for the top: Says Dan: "I like active sex, moving both of us around into different positions. This is a nice varia-tion—kind of porny and hot."

Benefit for the bottom: "Dan can get pretty vigorous," says Brent, "so in this position he can continue to fuck me and hold my leg up and get into it, but I can determine how deep he goes."

Extra credit: Adding new positions to your repertoire will have your partner wondering what new and amazing thing you'll do next.

Standing Back Door Position

The **Standing Back Door** is a favorite quickie position for Thomas, a single guy who is primarily a bottom. Thomas likes to bend forward and have his partner enter him from behind. It's easiest if Thomas bends pretty far forward to begin with (to straighten out the rectum), then he can straighten

up a bit after his playmate's penis is inside. Thomas is a fan of sex in semipublic places like airplane lavatories, and secluded spots in public parks. This position allows him just to drop his pants without getting fully undressed.

Benefit for the top: Says Thomas, "Most tops I'm with seem to think this position is really passionate—less like lovemaking and more like fucking. Guys get really animalistic when they know I want them to fuck me fast and hard."

Benefit for the bottom: "Who doesn't love a quickie?" says Thomas. "It's a pretty comfortable position, and I can play with my dick while the guy is ramming my butt. It's great for sex in the shower too."

Extra credit: If you're playing in a semipublic place, take off only as much clothing as you need to get access to your cocks and holes. Sometimes less disrobing is more exciting. (Don't get arrested!)

CHAPTER 7

Accoutrements:
Sex Toys and Accessories

★★

NO. 61 Toys for Boys

Sex toys are nothing new. The dildo, the granddaddy of sex toys, has been around for a few thousand years. Historical documents tell us the ancient Greeks used a pseudo-phallus they called an *olisbos*, which was made of stone, leather, or wood. In Renaissance Italy, *dilettos*—literally meaning, "delight"— were used with a generous sprinkling of olive oil. Some stuffy historians decided that these were items primarily used by single women—but don't you believe that for a minute! The ancient Greek and Italian men of the Renaissance (Alexander the Great, Leonardo da Vinci, and Michelangelo, for example) were pretty fond of sex with men. Consequently, my crack research staff has concluded that both gals and guys liked an occasional high hard one.

Thank goodness for modern technology. Not only do we no longer risk splinters (the term "wood" should really only be used figuratively), but there is now a seemingly endless array of shapes and designs, not only for dildos but for all kinds of toys that go in, on, and around your sensitive, tingly, naughty bits. Plus, sex toys never cheat on you.

Being the enlightened sexual beings we are, gay men know a few things about the use of sex toys (and if you don't already know a few things, read on). First, sex toys are not necessarily a replacement for human interaction. Sure, they can provide an extra zing during your solo play, but they can be used with another person as well. Using sex toys doesn't mean you'll become addicted to them and shun "the real thing," that is, sex with another human. Unless you have a highly addictive personality, sex toys will just enhance your sex life, not determine it.

Second, using toys doesn't necessarily mean that you're ultra hard-core and can't get off without a traffic cone up your ass. Having a few toys, or an entire closet full of them, does not indicate that you're a freak. So when you're getting comfortable (the naked kind of comfortable) with a new beau or a trick and he pulls out his stainless steel Vibrex 4000 ManWand, don't assume too much about him. He might be into hard-core kink, but he may also just like to play with a fun sex toy.

Third, sex toys, when used properly, will not damage your genitals or butt. The human body is remarkably resilient, so if you use common sense (and you stop your sex toy activities if whatever you're doing starts to hurt), you won't injure yourself.

When used properly, a good collection of toys can add excitement, variety, and even a sexy good dose of humor to your sex life.

Take a Trip to the Sex Store

Where to find these magical toys? These synthetic gateways to your pleasure centers? If you're in the boonies, just type "sex toys" into any Internet search engine and you'll get hundreds of links to retail sites that sell all kinds of toys for boys. If you live in a medium-size or larger city, you'll find that the place to go is the sex shop.

Once mostly the domain of sinister characters and dirty old men in raincoats, the sex shop has moved up in the world. The seedier shops with video booths are still around (and still very popular), but another kind of sex shop has emerged as well, especially in populous gay ghettos: the sex-positive stores that feature condoms, magazines, lube, sex toys, videos, gag gifts, sexy greeting cards, books, and other homo sundries. These newer, cleaner, more brightly lit shops (minus the porn "arcade") feature less wordless cruising and more friendly customer service—the legal kind. At shops that sell equipment for both hets and homos, you'll often find young couples of both persuasions shopping for videos and toys together, and young and old sexually liberated types searching for that perfect gift for a lover or for themselves. The staff is likely to thoughtfully answer your kink questions and even offer a knowledgeable suggestion or two.

So take a trip to your local sex shop for a little browsing. If you're apprehensive or embarrassed to go alone, take a friend. You'll probably find that it's not the scary place you imagined it to be—and if it is, look for a different store. If you're too shy to buy any goodies with your friend around, make mental notes on the equipment you want to try and return by yourself to make the purchases. If you're involved in a relationship, take your partner shopping for toys you'd like to try together. Deciding on a new toy together is a little less daunting than trying to find a way to casually introduce your new foot-long Cyberflesh dildo into precoital conversation.

If you're not fucking the person who came to the shop with you, you might consider refraining from buying the fire hydrant-size butt plug, the vat of lube with the foot pump, or the red leather cat-o'-nine-tails. Some things should be kept between you, the person you're flogging, and the sex store clerk. On the other hand, if your sex life is an open book, then by all means shop without hesitation.

You should probably purchase with cash rather than a credit card, just to avoid ending up on any mailing list. Don't expect to be able to return anything that doesn't quite fit wherever you're trying to shove it. Store policies range from a no-questions exchange for truly defective merchandise to a dirty look if you even mention trying to get your money back. Many better toys do have a warranty slip inside—but again, by filling it out you may end up on the manufacturer's catalog mailing list. There are plenty of shady companies putting out less than high-quality toys. As with so many other products, when you're buying sex toys, you usually get what you pay for. If it's cheap, it probably won't feel that great or last that long. So if you buy a $5 blow-up doll, you have only yourself to blame if it gets punctured easily and your stiffie deflates along with it.

No. 63 — Take Care of Your Toys

Part of being a modern-day gay Romeo means knowing about the different space-age materials you're playing with. Sex toys are composed of various man-made materials, each of which has its pros and cons. Look carefully at the packages of the toys you're buying; if the materials aren't indicated, ask a sales clerk. If he or she can't tell you what that fucshia two-headed dildo is made of, you might want to purchase something more readily identifiable. If the package does tell you what the product is made of, it might also give you instructions for the cleaning and storage of the toy. If it doesn't, well, you'll be glad you read the list below. Generally speaking, the softer the toy is, the more porous it is (the exception is silicone).

Silicone toys are nice and slippery. Nonporous, they're okay for guys who are allergic to latex, and they'll warm up just like you do. Being nonporous is good because that means the toy is less likely to hang on to bacteria or transmit STDs. Silicone toys are more expensive, but they're worth it. Do not use them with silicone-based lube—as we learned earlier, they're incompatible. These toys can be boiled or thrown in the dishwasher to be sterilized, or they can be washed with antibacterial soap and water. If you boil them, be sure the toys don't have any plastic parts that might melt.

Jelly toys are less expensive than silicone, but slightly stiffer and more porous. Because they are so porous, you might consider purchasing a sex-toy cleaning solution for these toys. Don't clean these toys with alcohol-based cleansers. Jelly toys stain easily (which can be more of a turnoff than a hygiene problem), so don't store light-colored jelly toys with your black toys, or wrap jelly toys in newspaper.

Cyberskin toys feel almost like human skin (which can be creepy in a sex toy) and they require a lot of care. Cyberskin is a very porous material and is damaged easily, so handle with care and follow the ritualistic cleaning instructions on the packaging. These toys need to be dusted with cornstarch after cleaning as well as a thorough drying to keep the surfaces from getting tacky.

Natural rubber latex is a popular material for condoms, dental dams, gloves, and some sex toys. Don't use latex toys with any oils (including oil-based lubes and foods containing oils), and don't use it if you're allergic to latex. Clean with antibacterial soap and water.

Synthetic rubber toys are plentiful, fairly soft, and conduct body heat. Clean them with antibacterial soap and water. They don't last very long, and they feel and smell like rubber. You can decide if that's a good thing.

Hard plastic toys are stiff, cheap, short-lived, plentiful, nonporous, and easy to clean. Use rubbing alcohol or antibacterial soap and water. File off any rough seams before use, or just cough up the extra cash for a better-made toy. Soft plastic toys are more porous, so use a cleaning product or a diluted bleach solution to keep them in good, safe condition.

Acrylic and **Lucite** are rock-hard, nonporous, and easy to clean with antibacterial soap and water. They're pretty, but they aren't particularly user-friendly because of their hardness, so a better place for your Lucite phallus might be your mantelpiece.

NO. 64 Stick It Where the Sun Don't Shine

Ah, the butt—a never-ending source of pleasure. While people can (and do) stick almost anything and everything up their chocolate whiz-ways, common sense dictates that some things are probably safer and more pleasurable than others. Putting household items like candles, cucumbers, or lightbulbs up your ass is ill advised. The lightbulb might break, and many a cucumber and candle has been lost up the ass of a zealous butt-play fan. I suggest shelling out the wampum for a well-made toy. Ass toys come in four main varieties: dildos, butt plugs, vibrators, and anal beads. We'll start with the penis-shaped toys.

Dildos are phalluses made of latex, plastic, rubber, Lucite, or silicone. They're most often inserted anally as an aid to masturbation. Standard-issue dildos look like erect penises. Some are smooth cylinders with a rounded end; others are more lifelike and often shaped like actual cocks— complete with veins and a distinct glans. They come in various sizes, from wee pinkie-shaped probes to mammoth schlongs of enormously exaggerated proportions. In general you should look for pliable dildos rather than rigid ones. Some are bendable, and many even include a suction cup on the base that allows them to be stuck to a floor or wall. You can literally go fuck yourself while the suction cup keeps the dong firmly in place.

Sex shops sell "celebrity" dildos modeled after porn star dicks—though calling a porn star a celebrity is perhaps a bit of hyperbole. The box may claim that a porn-star dildo is "actual size," but trust me, it's an exaggeration. They are not actual size; in fact, they're inflated to superhuman dimensions. But what the hell do you care? You still get a big, veiny cock to put up your ass, and you've paid for the privilege of pretending it's the cock of a virile, horse-hung, 22-year-old Czech stud.

Double-headed dildos usually come in lengths of 12, 14, or 18 inches and allow you and a partner to get fucked up the ass simultaneously. Using double-headed dildos takes a little coordination (arranging the right position, timing your thrusts, etc.) but can be a great option for bottom guys playing together, or for versatile guys looking for a new experience. Pick a model that includes balls or a flared middle so the dildo can't slip all the way inside either partner.

Vibrators are dildos with a little extra mojo. They most often appear as battery-powered or plug-in models. Nonvibrating dildos are arguably more common in the toy chests of gay men than vibrators are, but if you like a little vroom in your back room, then consider investing in a quality vibrator. Vibrators can also be used for stimulation on bits other than your ass. Hold them on the perineum or balls for a very special sensation.

Cover the vibrator with a nonlubricated or water-based lubed condom before use. As with all butt play, using these devices requires attention to cleanliness, patience, and plenty of warm-up play for the butt. Never share your butt toys without cleaning them thoroughly first. Yes, I know your mother taught you to share, but she'll understand if you don't use your dildo on a play-mate without a good cleaning first. Or you can just skip telling your mom about it.

NO. 65 Toys That Teach You to Take It Like a Man

Butt plugs are dildos with a bulging middle section and a flared base. They are meant to be inserted and worn for a certain period of time—minutes or a few hours, Sparky, not days. The flared base stays outside your asshole, which keeps the plug from slipping all the way inside.

They're not designed to be thrust in and out of your tush. The flared middle is meant to give you that sense of fullness (and by "fullness," I mean the feeling of a cock up your butt) and to keep the butt plug anchored in your rectum and not swimming up through your colon.

Butt plugs are good for training novice bottoms too. Since a butt plug can be inserted when you're alone, you can pop it in, get used to the feeling, and then pop it out when you're ready for some hot sodomy with a pal (now legal in all 50 U.S. states). Using a butt plug can help you learn to control the contractions of your sphincter and to distinguish between the feeling of being fucked and needing to use the toilet. Plus, since butt plugs keep your ass open just a little bit, if you wear one for a while before anal sex, you'll be more receptive.

Pliable plugs stimulate the prostate as you move around or sit down. Since no one has to know you're wearing one, they can be a great dirty little secret if you use one when you're at the grocery store, on car trips, or at a dinner party. Some vibrating models now come with a remote-control unit. Give the remote to a friend who can control the vibrating function at random wherever you are. Standing in line at the post office was never so much fun.

Anal beads are a series of large molded plastic beads, often strung together on a nylon cord. The string usually has a pull handle at one end. Some guys prefer the sensation of inserting them in one at a time (hold the string slightly taut as you insert them), while for other guys the payoff is pulling them out right before or during orgasm to trigger anal spasms that can make an orgasm last longer. If you're lending a hand, do *not* yank on the string! It is not an outboard motor or lawn mower cord. Pulling the beads out too quickly will make his asshole really angry and you might never be invited back inside.

The safest kind of anal beads are those where the entire apparatus has been dipped in latex, silicone, or rubber so that the coating on the beads actually covers the string too. It saves you from an otherwise difficult cleanup. Other types of anal beads are connected by a flexible rod so they're a bit easier to insert and remove.

NO. 66

Ring Around the Cock

Cock rings are simple devices that wrap around the base of your penis and/or scrotum, to intensify your erection. They can be used during masturbation, oral sex or fucking. Most are made of metal, leather, rubber, or cloth, and come in two varieties: adjustable and solid. You can put on an adjustable cock ring when your dick is hard or soft. Just wrap the ring around the base of your cock and balls, then fasten it shut (most adjustable rings have snaps or Velcro). Adjust the tightness as needed.

You must be flaccid to put on a solid-metal or rubber cock ring. First, put your balls through the ring, then your dick. Cock rings work by restricting the flow of blood out of your one-eyed bandit. During an erection, more blood flows in than flows out, and the spongy tissues in the shaft fill with blood, making you hard. Because your veins are closer to the surface of your dick than your arteries are, cock rings make you even harder by further restricting the outward blood flow.

The best cock rings are made of leather, cloth, or another flexible material. Because you must be soft to put on a solid cock ring, you must also be soft to remove it. And because the solid cock rings keep you hard indefinitely, you might have trouble getting your erection to go down sufficiently to get the ring off. While having a rock-hard dick for hours at a time sounds like a good thing, it isn't. You risk cutting off your circulation, and nasty things can start to happen when you cut off the oxygenated blood supply to your favorite appendage.

Suffice it to say that neophytes should stick to the adjustable kind—and experiment with the amount of time the cock ring is worn. If your dick starts to burn, tingle, or get numb, you should take the cock ring off immediately. An ice pack can help deflate you, but if you're stuck in a cock ring after a couple of hours, get to an emergency room to have it cut off before your dick falls off.

Cock rings are very popular with men who experience some occasional erectile dysfunction or whose partying habits include drugs that make them horny but also take the snap out of their turtles. Other men don't need them to get hard but just like the look or sensation of an extra-hard dick. Justin, a 28-year-old café waiter in Fort Lauderdale, says, "I have no trouble getting it up. I just like the look of cock rings. And I like wearing a fairly loose one under my clothes when I'm at work. It feels a little dirty, plus it makes my package look bigger. And my crotch is just about table-top height when I'm taking an order."

Don't have an adjustable leather cock ring or a solid metal ring? A strap of leather that can be tied in place can work just as well, as can a shoelace or nylon cord. Any of these materials can be easily cut off, if they become too tight or difficult to untie. Silicone cock rings are also good for novices. They look a little bit like gummi candy, but they can stretch to several times their original size for easy application and removal. A little lube and some precision manscaping can keep you from getting hairs yanked out by the snaps on an adjustable cock ring or a solid rubber ring.

NO. 67

Tit Clamps—Not Just for Tit Mice Anymore

Nipple clamps (also called tit clamps) are not nearly as scary as they appear. A novice's apprehension is understandable—the things are usually metal and are often connected by chain. They definitely look more S/M than vanilla. But kinky is really just a state of mind, so if you enjoy nipple play—anywhere from gentle tweaking to serious tit torture—you'll find they can add a little bit of hot sauce to your sexual recipe book. Call it "hot vanilla," if it makes you feel better.

The main purpose of nipple clamps is not to pinch your nipples into painful nubs, but to provide the constant pressure that increases sensitivity. Tit clamps can provide the stimulation you desire while keeping your hands free to stroke your dick, play with his butt, work the pulleys, or don the hand puppets—whatever it is you need your hands for. Good nipple clamps are more than modified clothespins. They're adjustable for desired pressure, and the bits that touch your tits are padded with cork, vinyl, or rubber. This padding will keep them in place and protect your nipples.

Alligator clamps are little spring-loaded contraptions with a locking mechanism that allows you to set the tension to a desired level. There are also simple tweezer clamps with a metal band that you can slide up or down to adjust the pressure. Another scissors-shaped variety of clamp works well with your doctor/male nurse/patient fantasies (it will look familiar if you've ever seen *ER*. Again, they have a locking device to keep them in place, but you'll need a set of two—one for each nipple.

A simple chain can be added to keep the clamps together, and you can tug on the chain to stimulate both nipples simultaneously. The metal lends to the whole affair a fetish look, which can play into an S/M scene. (The dominant guy can lead the submissive guy around by his nipple chain.)

Your titties are made of delicate tissue, so make sure you start slowly, and use the clamps for no more than 15 to 20 minutes at a time, until you know how your body responds. Start conservatively and tighten slowly. If the toy is spring-loaded, do not let it snap shut. Once you've trapped your titties, light touches or brushing up against the clamp will send waves of pleasure throughout your body. The clamps can be modified by attaching weights or a special vibrator to each clamp.

Make sure to remove the clamps immediately if you feel pain, or if the skin gets broken or discolored. If your nips are already pierced, take out any hardware before applying clamps, or position the clamps so that they don't smash your flesh against the metal you already have. When you remove the clamps, blood will rush back to your tits, so you might feel a slightly painful sensation. If you overdo it with your new clamps, apply some ice to reduce the swelling.

Have a Stroke
Like you need any help with masturbating, right? A little variety never hurt any-

one, and with a bit of lube and a little imagination, a synthetic stroke device can aid in that ages-old ritual by adding a different twist to your he-bop.

The basic **masturbation sleeve** is a silicone or jelly tube that fits over your erect lubed penis. The interior is often covered with soft tiny nubs or ridges that tickle your dick as you slide it up and down. Just lube, grip, jerk, and shoot!

The newest masturbation sleeves have Cyberskin interiors. The business ends of these high-tech toys are variously shaped like mouths or assholes, and come in different sizes and colors. Because Cyberskin is so stretchy, the aperture in these newer devices might not appear to accommodate your dick. We all occasionally fantasize about being able to say, "Heh, heh—my big dick won't fit in there!" But with a little lube, it probably will slide in just fine.

The more elaborate masturbation devices are modeled to look like an entire face or hindquarters (sometimes with hands reaching back to hold the ass cheeks open for you—thoughtful, no?). The more intricate ones are shaped to accommodate particular fetishes, like women's strappy shoes.

Take care, though: Jelly and Cyberskin are delicate and susceptible to rips and tears that will expand quickly. They tend to get slick after a coating of lube, so keep a towel handy to wipe off your hands and the sleeve. Because the interior tube will have lube and/or your spunk in it, make sure to clean it thoroughly with antibacterial soap and dry it completely before putting it away.

NO. 69

The Rough Stuff

Thanks to family-friendly events like the Folsom Street Fair, leatherman competitions across the country and around the world, and those wacky *Police Academy* movies, the BDSM (bondage/discipline/sadomasochism) lifestyle has become well-known for certain imagery: leather harnesses, chaps, hats, whips, metal chains, and cigars. We'll take a closer look at S/M and fantasy role-play in Secret #82, but in the meantime, here are a few tips for picking the proper bondage tools to get you started on the road to kinksville.

Regarding **handcuffs:** Only cops use the real thing. Die-hard bondage enthusiasts know that the real McCoy are *pain* cuffs—and we're not talking about a good, slap-my-ass-and-call-me-a-bad-boy kind of pain. True police handcuffs are designed to be very tight and to minimize prisoner activity during transport. Misuse can cause nerve and bone damage, which would suck, especially if you're only after some hot bondage play. If you've got a pair of the real thing, use them for show, never for sex play. Consult your local S/M shop (if you live near a gay ghetto) or your local sex shop for some suggestions on more suitable sex-friendly handcuffs.

When you use any kind of restraints, make sure they aren't too tight. The bound guy should be able to move his wrists freely in the cuffs and he should not rest or be positioned on his cuffed hands, or be dragged around by the cuffs. Better handcuff brands have a locking mechanism that prevents them from tightening after you've cuffed your prisoner.

Rope can be found in great varieties at your local hardware store, and can be great for tying each other to your four-poster bed, Princess, or for a little bondage play (more on that in Secret #88). Cotton clothesline works well too, and it's thick and soft enough not to cut into delicate skin. Similarly, nylon rope is smooth, strong, and unlikely to cause chafing. Stay away from scratchy materials like twine (it's thin and it can cut skin) and hemp (very scratchy). Neckties and scarves work well for tying up a willing partner because they are skin-friendly, but don't use anything you're unwilling to sacrifice if you need to cut him loose. Break out that old Boy Scout manual for some instruction on tying the knots. Stay away from nylons or panty hose (not that you have any around the house, you butch thing, you) because they can get too tight and cut off circulation.

Bondage beginners might try **padded leather cuffs** that fit snuggly around wrists and ankles. These cuffs have little metal rings to which rope can be tied, rather than directly to the skin, so there's no resulting skin irritation. There are also beginner bondage kits that feature **Velcro restraints,** which should keep you pleasantly immobile but can come loose when necessary. It's best to keep things simple until you've got some experience under your belt.

NO. 70

We're Here to Pump (Clap) You Up!

Penis pumps will not make your dick any bigger. Well, a pump will make your penis bigger than it is when it's flaccid because the pump produces an erection. But when your petunia droops again, it will be the same as it was yesterday. Abandon all delusions, ye who enter here. Penis pumps—which usually consist of a sealed tube, a gasket to create a seal around the base of your dick, and a hand-powered pump—look more like retro medical devices than sex toys. They were initially designed for men with erectile problems to help them get it up prior to intercourse. By placing the pump over your dick and pumping the air out, you create a vacuum. Blood rushes into your dick, and your dick gets bigger, creating an erection.

Some practitioners use the pumps on their penises and on their scrotum. A Web search for "penis pumps" will produce a series of sites with pictures of hugely inflated ball sacs and distended dicks. It's entirely up to you whether you think the images are sexy. I tend to think they look like painful examples of lymphatic filariasis from medical manuals, but then again, "sexy" is subjective.

So pump at your own peril. There is no scientific evidence that any permanent size increase occurs from pumping your dick. The (addlebrained?) theory goes that the regular use of a pump is similar to weight lifting: Repeated use will stretch your erectile tissue so your erect dick gets bigger over time. Once again I ask you, dear reader, to repeat after me: *The penis is not a muscle. My cock is the perfect size as it is. I will not subject my favorite appendage to bruising, burst capillaries, and blistering in an ill-advised effort to make it bigger. I will not foolishly cause damage to my love wand that might permanently prevent me from achieving erections naturally. Amen.*

Nevertheless, plenty of guys swear by them, so if you're determined to use a penis pump, try to find a reliable source of information on how to proceed with caution. That source of information would not be someone trying to sell you a pump. As long as you tread cautiously and occasionally use pumps for solo sex or a little bit of exhibitionism (and not to try to make your dick bigger), you will be fine. Just don't expect miracles. By no means should you ever, ever, *ever* use a household vacuum cleaner anywhere near your dangler. As I warned you earlier: You'll take the skin off. No fun and not pretty.

CHAPTER 8

How to Play Better With Others

****

NO. 71

Dude, You Need a Home Sex Kit

By now you've learned how to whip yourself into a masturbatory frenzy, give a head-spinning blow job, fuck and get fucked like a paid professional, and dozens of other techniques that will keep you on top of your game and keep the guys coming back for more. But your charm and prodigious technique aren't the be-all and end-all to a great time in the sack. You need to set the proper environment for lovin'—or a reasonable facsimile thereof.

Take a cue from Martha Stewart by keeping a few things in good supply at your home. You'll always be ready to go when your seduction techniques at the bar or grocery store pay off. And it will ensure you're ready for surprise sex too—you don't want to turn down a hot porno-plot sexperience with the sexy UPS guy or cable man just because you're not stocked up on supplies when he comes knocking. The hunt for condoms—though it's the plot of many crappy B-movies—is a major wood-kill in real life. If you leave a trouserless man alone in your house or apartment while you go to the drugstore, chances are your afternoon delight will have evaporated by the time you get back. The UPS guy has more packages to deliver, after all.

Below are the basics for a home sex kit. Keep these basic items handy and you'll be equipped for an afternoon quickie or a marathon all-night love-in.

Lube: Water-based for safe sex play, and maybe oil-based for yourself (if you like the sensation better) or for him too if you're just going to jerk off, not fuck.

Condoms: Nonlubricated latex is your best bet, but water-based lubed condoms are okay too. If you're allergic to latex, get some polyurethane condoms. Keep a supply in a size that fits you. Since wishful thinking never hurt anyone, keep a few large-size condoms around too. If you're partial to freebies, keep a handy stash of the complimentary condoms you can pick up at many gay bars and clubs. Keep all your rubbers in one place. Nothing says "I'm a hoochie" like having condoms in every drawer in the house.

Dark-colored towels: Whether you're playing on the couch, kitchen floor, or your bed, keep one or two dark-colored towels handy for quick and easy cleanup. Why dark towels? They reduce the "ick" factor if anal sex gets a little messy. Whatever you use, don't offer him the crusty, come-stained sweat sock you use for solo squirting. Keep that dirty little secret to yourself.

Soap and shampoo: Keep your bathroom countertop stocked with some antibacterial soap for hands when you only need a light cleanup, and keep a bottle of unscented body wash in the shower in case either of you needs a more thorough scrub down. For showers, a squeeze bottle or one with a pump top is the most user-friendly for boys with sticky fingers. Keep some shampoo around too. You don't have to offer him your expensive imported jojoba and essence-of-avocado-seed shampoo, if you're fussy about that kind of thing. A bottle of unscented store brand will do the trick for a trick.

Basic toiletries: If the sexy plumber does drop in to inspect your pipe, he may need to be presentable by the time he leaves the house. Some face and body moisturizer (you should use them daily too), hair product, and deodorant will suffice. Planning on any overnight visitors? Keeping an extra toothbrush around, unopened from its packaging, is a nice touch. If you prefer to buy in bulk, hide the 50-count box of toothbrushes you keep around for horny houseguests. One can *be* a slut, but one should never *look* like a slut.

NO. 72 The Way to a Man's Heart

There are times when the last thing in the world you want is for the guy you just got off with to stick around. Other times, you'll want to woo the man who made you goo. Nothing says "stick around" after a night of testing the bedsprings like some good old-fashioned hospitality. Plenty of guys are nervous about the kind of intimacy that comes with talking face-to-face with a guy in the full light of day the morning after—the morning after you've cruised him, wowed him with your wiles, got him into your bed, and made him howl like a wolf because of your tremendous sexual technique. But don't be afraid. After all, if you've had his cock down your throat, what's wrong with looking him in the eye? If you want him to stick around, or if you're hoping to see him a second time (maybe even in daylight), now's a great chance to make him feel like he's the only guy in the world.

Being hospitable the morning after starts with coffee or tea. Most guys drink one or the other, and since you can't guess which (or maybe you'll bed both coffee and tea drinkers), it's best to keep both on hand. It's also good to have some juice, some bread, jam or preserves, eggs, and some fresh fruit around as well. Those are the fixings for a basic breakfast that anyone can whip together in a few minutes. You'll win instant points by offering to make him some grub as he's rolling nakedly out of your bed. Yes, that means you should get up first.

Guys who know how to cook are sexy—whip up some eggs while wearing nothing but an apron. Whether you are a gourmet or just a fast-food connoisseur, you should definitely know how to toast bread, slice up some fruit, and scramble some eggs or make a quickie omelet. Breakfast can be the simplest meal to make, and your effort will go a long way toward impressing him.

In addition to knowing a breakfast dish or two, you should know how to put together three or four dinner dishes with some level of competence. A candlelit dinner can be the prelude to a night of romance, and romance can be the lead-in to some serious slap-and-tickle. If you're uneasy cooking for a fella, the same friends that you plied with margaritas to dissect your wardrobe will probably be happy to be your culinary guinea pigs in exchange for a free meal.

Easy yet swanky dishes include main courses like linguini puttanesca, baked salmon with dill, grilled steaks or chicken (grilling is very butch), a homemade pizza margherita with fresh mozzarella and basil, and pan-fried pork chops with chutney. Believe it or not, even foods that sound complicated, like Thai and Mexican dishes, are totally easy after a practice run or two, and the ingredients are available at any large grocery store. Pick up a beginner's cookbook or flip on any of the thousands of cooking shows that fill the airwaves and give it a go. Still have no idea what to cook? Take notes next time you're out at a restaurant and then go home and look up a recipe online. Free recipes are everywhere on the Internet.

Pick dishes that are seasonally appropriate (for example, avoid hot soups in midsummer), and if your recipe calls for fresh fruits and veggies, make sure they're in season or attempt another dish. Pick out a bottle of complimentary wine—any clerk at a wine store can steer you in the right direction if you have questions. Be careful to avoid white zinfandels and anything in a box. Now make that date.

NO. 73

Get to Know the Other Swizzle Sticks

A nice wine or imported or microbrew beer accompanies most meals nicely, but on occasions when you aren't cooking a full meal, you should know how to prepare a few adult cocktails for gentlemen callers. That big blue sugary drink special with the parasol straw you liked to order at bars when you were 21 was great for getting you fucked up fast, but it didn't come off as particularly grown-up. You just didn't care then. But now, unless you're throwing a theme party, don't offer to make your date a mai tai, a zombie, or a Singapore sling.

Cocktails styles change with the times, just like fashion. It makes sense to keep up with trends, but the classics are never out of style. You couldn't get through a crowded bar in Los Angeles in the last three years without having a drunk queen spill his green apple martini on your shoes. Martinis are still in vogue in various fruity incarnations, but a traditional gin or vodka martini is worth knowing how to make. So are gin and tonics with lime, Cape Cods, screwdrivers, and a few top-shelf liquors on the rocks. And if you can make a good Bloody Mary, you'll have friends for life.

A really well-stocked bar will have vodka, gin, whiskey, rum, tequila, cola, tonic water, soda water, dry vermouth, olives, limes, lemons, ice, juice mixers, and whatever other liquors and mixers you're fond of. A slightly skimpier but still functional bar can include juice mixers, tonic, vodka (it goes well with most mixers), whisky or rum, ice, cola, lemons and limes.

Keep a decent bottle of red wine (at just below room temperature) on hand too, and a bottle of chilled white wine. Remember: No white zinfandels! Anything you serve chilled should remain cool but not cold while you're storing it. Moving alcohol from refrigeration to room temperature and back again will ruin the flavor.

A well-stocked cupboard includes a variety of serving glasses to accentuate the beverage you're serving. The basics include wine glasses in several shapes (big round "balloons" for red wine, regular shaped wine glasses for white wine, flutes for champagne); martini glasses for martinis; tall "highball" glasses for mixed cocktails with ice; and shorter "old-fashioned" glasses for liquor only or liquor on ice. Highball glasses and regular wineglasses are fine if they're all you've got, but we're talking about making a good impression, right? Consider splurging and get a set of each of the above. Save the jelly jars and plastic tumblers for when you're drinking that hooch alone while watching Lifetime Television. Other bar necessities include a bottle opener, a corkscrew, a long spoon for stirring, a martini shaker, and a jigger for measuring alcohol.

A quick rundown of cocktail terms will keep you on your toes so that when you offer your date a drink, he doesn't throw you a curve ball. "Neat" means liquor served in an old-fashioned without ice. "A twist" is a curl of lemon peel (not a whole wedge) served in a drink. "On the rocks" means liquor served over ice. "Bottoms up" means...well, that one's up to you.

NO. 74

Good Bedding for Bedding Him

One way to make him want to stay all night in your bed is to have a decent bed. Just like you ditched the *Star Wars* bedspread when you were 14, you should ditch the mix-and-match and partial sets of sheets and pillowcases and scrap all the hand-me-down beddings you lifted from your parents' linen closet (or secretly smuggle them back). If you're still sleeping on a futon, or if your mattress is on the floor instead of on a bed frame, it's time to invest in some better furnishings. A futon, or a bed with threadbare, stained, or mismatched sheets, screams "financial instability" (or "cooties!").

Invest in some matching sheets with a nice high thread count. You don't have to spend thousands of dollars on designer Egyptian cotton sheets, but get something that is reasonably nice and matches your tastes—and your other bedding. When in doubt, neutrals are usually pretty good choices for colors. They're always in style and they're masculine. Always use a mattress pad under your fitted sheets.

Aside from being the main romper room, your bedroom should be a sanctuary, especially if you have roommates. Pick colors that you like but leave the fussy floral designs alone, even if you think they look manly enough for you. At best they become dated quickly, and at worst they look creepy, like you might also have a collection of porcelain dolls hidden in a secret room somewhere. When designing your boudoir, think of the big picture: Your sexual credibility and the design reputation of all homos is on the line. One badly designed bedroom can ruin it for us all.

And while you're at it, ditch the posters, the beer-bottle collections, the milk carton furniture, and any stuffed animals that were gifts from boyfriends past. Take all photos of old boyfriends off the wall and put them into an album that you can tuck away. No one needs to be reminded that they're "next."

Hair Today...Red Itchy Bumps Tomorrow?

Few topics polarize gay men more than the question of body hair. But whether you like body hair or despise it, there are definite advantages to some selective manscaping. Trimming your chest and stomach hair with a set of clippers can emphasize a good physique and minimize the appearance of a big belly. Carefully trimming the bush around your dick can make your shlong look longer—and who doesn't want that?

Even some hirsute guys occasionally like to have their back hair and shoulder hair removed. I'm not saying anyone *should* remove body hair. Lord knows I don't need letters from bear clubs and fur fans sent to my house. But for both hairy bears and waxed gym bunnies and everyone in between, there's no excuse for tufts of hair sprouting from your nose or ears. Such hair is always bad. *Bad!* So take a good look in the mirror, grab the tweezers (and maybe a shot of tequila to dull the pain), and trim or pluck it now!

For the rest of your body, should you wish to remove

hair, you can trim it, shave it, tweeze it, electrocute it, laser it, or wax it. Gay men are pioneers, and perhaps in no field is our impact more keenly felt than in the domain of hair removal. Okay, maybe we have made other more important contributions. I know there's no Nobel Prize waiting for us for removal of unwanted body hair, but heterosexual men with a penchant for expensive Italian loafers have us to thank for paving the way for them in yet another arena: They can now go into a salon and ask for an ass waxing with a straight face.

Here are a few grooming tips for the different spots on your body. These are at-home or simple salon techniques that don't involve electricity or laser beams.

Face: Shaving is your only option, and doing it immediately after a shower is best because hair absorbs water and will yield to a razor more easily when it's wet. Let the shaving cream sit on your face and neck for a couple of minutes before shaving. This will further soften your beard. Shave in the same direction as your hair growth pattern—not against it. Don't ever wax your face. It can cause serious skin irritation.

Eyebrows: Stick to tweezing. While it's possible to wax your eyebrows, waxed brows on boys tend to look overly manicured. Using fine-nosed tweezers in a straight, sharp movement will pull the hair cleanly from the roots.

Back of the neck: It should be shaved or clippered. Waxing is a no-no here.

Underarms: Waxing and shaving are safe here. Because the hair grows in all different directions, it makes little difference if you shave up or down or side to side. Don't use deodorant or antiperspirants immediately afterward. No depilatories!

Shoulders and back: Shaving is not advisable because the regrowth will result in painful ingrown hairs. Wax or use clippers on the areas. Taking a shower immediately after waxing helps minimize redness and breakouts.

Chest and stomach: Waxing works well, but don't shower immediately before waxing. Water softens the hair, but tough hair comes off better in waxing. Clippering works well, and shaving can work well but you may develop ingrown hairs. If you must shave your chest, shower first and let the shaving cream sit on it for two or three minutes. Splash with cold water after shaving to minimize bleeding from minor cuts. Wash well with soap and water to reduce the risk of infection, and follow up with rubbing alcohol or shaving lotion. After 24 hours, exfoliate with a loofah to prevent dead skin cells from clogging follicles and causing ingrown hair. To avoid slicing off your nipples, stick to tweezers to remove hair there.

Genitals: Trimming with scissors (watch the blades, Buster), clippering, and careful shaving are all okay. You can eliminate hair growing on the shaft of your penis with a new, wet razor, and a slow, steady hand. Your testicles can be shaved as well, but make sure you use a new razor and clear the blade of hair after each stroke. Don't try depilatories unless you like the feeling of rug burn on your balls.

NO. 76 Overnight Etiquette

Should he stay the night? If what you're planning is just a sex date and your fuck buddy is familiar with the routine, there's no need for a sleepover. He knows he's coming over for a blow job—maybe some ass, maybe not—and then he's out the door. This is the kind of thing that you should firmly establish before he arrives.

If you have invited a date over—someone you'd like to see again in public, maybe someone you'd eventually like to introduce to your parents—you don't want to have any post-sex embarrassment by stammering out a reason why he has to clean up, pull on his pants, and hit the road. He may decide you just want him for a fuck buddy. Or worse, he may decide that you're just a classless oaf whom he'd rather not see again. Don't burn bridges by pissing off guys you like. A little communication can easily solve this problem.

If you're inviting someone over and sex is on the menu, you should indicate clearly—*before he crosses your threshold*—whether he's invited to stay the night. A simple "I'd love for you to stay the night" is concise, polite, and leaves no room for confusion. Plus it can be very sexy too. Spooning with someone and the potential for morning sex is an enticement many men can't refuse. But then, maybe his welcome is short-lived—maybe he snores, or maybe you're drunk and not quite sure what he'll look like in the glaring light of day. Or maybe he *is* just a fuck buddy, but he doesn't know it yet. If you don't want there when you wake up, you'd better have a good reason for not inviting him to stay over *before he enters your home.* An important appointment usually works well as a reason. Even if he sees through your flimsy excuse, he'll probably get the drift. "I've got an early squash game tomorrow" would have worked, if you were a 1980s coke-snorting Wall Street type, but it's a little passé now, so you'll have to come up with a better excuse. Try "the plumber is coming early" (*and the plumber is an Adonis*—don't say that part) or "I've got to get to an early appointment for work." Both should suffice. If he's not driving his own car, offer to pick up the tab for his ride home.

This rule is merely an etiquette guideline. And being a matter of politeness, the rule goes both ways. If he invites you to his place and you'd rather not spend the night—maybe he's got a futon and mismatched sheets—give him the same kind of good reason for not spooning with him.

In either case—whether you stay or go, whether he stays or goes—if one of you has an orgasm, the other one should too before you part ways. Feelings get hurt easily over the idea of mutual satisfaction, especially when there's potential for a real emotional connection. Don't be greedy by withholding your own orgasm. If he comes, you should too; otherwise, he may come up with many unfounded reasons why he didn't make you spurt. It can be an ego blow—the bad kind.

Don't waste any time on a steady date who doesn't invite you to stay overnight, or who doesn't accept your offer for him to stay, after two or three sexual encounters. And stay away from anyone who gives you flimsy excuses for you not being able to go to his place—ever. He clearly just wants a sex buddy, or he's closeted, or a drug dealer, or has intimacy issues, or whatever. He's too messed up for you to bother with. Curb him, and while you're at it (and for the sake of the next guy he dates), tell him why you're dropping him.

NO. 77

Three-way Etiquette
A ménage à trois can be a mind-blowing sexual encounter. It can also provoke an emotional response that might

not happen if you were just having sex with one other person—especially if two of the three participants are in a relationship together. So if you find yourself with two hot guys pawing at your swimsuit area and you want to jump in, go into the situation with a clear understanding of what a three-way entails. When it goes smoothly, a three-way can mean extra hands, extra throbbing cocks, extra ass cheeks, extra mouths. More is more, right? When it doesn't go well, a three-way can be a big festering pile of resentment and hurt feelings. Go for it if the idea turns you on, but head in with open eyes.

A threesome most often happens when a gay couple invites a third guy into their bedroom. Three-way sex between three unattached guys can happen, but the meeting is a little harder to orchestrate. Gay couples, even devoted ones, are a liberated species. They're not limited to proper "couples," as many nesting hetero couples are. Gay couples go to bars, clubs, dinner parties, art openings, circuit parties, even sex clubs and bathhouses. Almost any place that gay singles go, gay couples go. And gay couples are often (though not always) less rigid than heterosexual couples in their notions of fidelity. The result can mean guys who play outside of their relationships, or couples who play together with a third guy (or gal), or couples who play in a group but only when both partners are present, or a partner who turns a blind eye to his mate's extracurricular sex play. The permutations are endless. If you're in the couple and interested in a three-way, lay out your ground rules about sex with a third guy before the third guy even crosses your path. If you're the third guy, ask a little bit about the couple's arrangement. Knowing how they think about sex in their relationship can save you from sticking your foot in your mouth or sticking your dick where it doesn't belong. If your questions offend them, move on.

In situations where a couple invites a third guy in, the couple usually has an understanding that they're both interested in having sex with the third guy. If you're invited to go home with a couple, you should be prepared for the psychosexual landscape you're entering. Chances are you'll be attracted to one man more than you are to the other. That's no one's fault; it's a matter of human nature. Good three-way etiquette dictates that you not indicate you like one over the other because it can make one man feel excluded. When a couple takes you home to play, sex is at the top of the agenda, so dispense with the chitchat you'd engage in on a one-on-one date and get down to business.

Three-ways with three unattached guys are less frequent, but they can be a blast nonetheless. Don't enter a ménage à trois if one of the other two guys is someone you're interested in dating. His first sexual impression of you should not be the one of you with two cocks in your mouth.

The mechanics of a three-way are endless: two cocks in one mouth; a three-way suckfest; one cock up your ass while you suck the other guy; fucking one guy while he's getting sucked; fucking while getting fucked (you Lucky Pierre, you); taking turns watching while the other two play. Here's where an ample supply of lube, condoms, and fun sex toys can keep you busy for hours. Just follow your imagination. Three-ways don't come along every day for most guys, so it's your duty to explore as many possible configurations as your stamina will allow. Safe sex requires extra diligence in group play, however.

If you're in a couple and doing the hosting, offer your guest a shower afterward, plenty of towels, and then thank him for coming over and coming all over you. Don't feel obligated to offer him the bed to stay over. There's no real comfortable way for any three men to sleep in one bed together. If you're the third and they ask you to stay, expect morning sex too. After all, that's the primary reason you're there.

NO. 78 Take It on the Road

Just like keeping your house or apartment stocked with the necessary supplies for an overnight date or unexpected rendezvous, today's modern man should be able to take his show on the road. Having a few choice items in a travel bag that you can quickly pick up and throw in the car can make a little outdoor rendezvous possible.

As the old joke goes: What do you do when you come across a hot hitchhiker? Wipe him off, of course. Jokes and hitchhiker serial killer stories aside, you never know when you're going to encounter a sex-ready situation. Unprotected, nonlubed sex is nobody's idea of a picnic, so why not pack a kit so you're prepared for any eventuality? Say you're hiking in a public park or a national forest and you suddenly stumble upon a seriously hot guy whom you wouldn't mind giving an all-over tongue bath. If he gives you some eye contact back, you might have a playmate on your hands. You'll want to be prepared. Likewise, if you and your boyfriend find that a little action in the backseat of your car is a bit more exciting than in your bedroom, you'll need the proper equipment for a little mobile fun.

Keep these items in a travel bag in the trunk of your car and you'll never be caught with your pants down (figuratively) when you want your take your pants down (literally).

Condoms: A few nonlubed or water-based lubed condoms will keep you protected when you're with a buddy—whether on a cross-country road trip or just across town—and suddenly you feel the urge for a bit of tail. (Make sure to park where you can't be seen.)

Lube: Sex shops and gay video stores usually sell lube in (confoundingly tough-to-open) mini packets. One packet is just the right size for a solo stroke in the brambles or behind a rest stop on the interstate, and two packets is plenty for fucking around with a new friend in the back of your car.

Blanket: Sex in a field or on the beach is hot, no matter how you slice it, but you're likely to want to do it longer if you don't have sand scraping your sensitive bits and briars and reeds poking you when you're poking him. Lay down a blanket first and voilá!—you have an instant boudoir.

Wet naps: Regular road-trippers will tell you to keep them handy for cleaning up after a meal on the go, but dirty birdies know that cleanup after sex is even easier when you've got a jumbo-size bottle of premoistened towelettes in your car.

NO. 79 Bathhouse Etiquette

Public bathhouses have been around for centuries, as far back as ancient Greece and Rome, and even then, getting clean wasn't all those guys had in mind. But bathhouses designed specifically as places for gay men to meet and have sex are a more recent invention, starting in the early 20th century in major cities in Europe and the United States. Then and now, the major attraction of the bathhouse has been no-strings sex with more safety than cruising parks or public areas.

Venues vary in decor, cleanliness, and clientele, so if you're in a big city with a few options, look in the local gay paper or ask around to determine if the place you're interested in caters to your tastes. Are the clientele collegiate or daddy types? Do the guys like to cruise and watch or just get down to it? What days and times are busiest?

Most establishments have a similar setup: You'll pay an admission fee, and you'll be given a towel and a condom. You'll be able to rent a locker to store your clothes and valuables, or you can rent a small room with a bed and a lock on the door. Sometimes you'll be able to check your valuables at the door for safekeeping. You can expect showers, steam rooms, dry saunas, a Jacuzzi or swimming pool, private rooms, a TV room with porno playing, and occasionally mazes or dark rooms.

Most often, a guy will disrobe, stow his clothes, wrap a towel around his waist, take a shower, and go stroll around the place. Guys will be wandering the halls and some will be waiting in rooms with the doors opened.

Neil, a 29-year-old law clerk in Toronto, has been to bathhouses a few times, mostly when he's on vacation in another city. "Bathhouse etiquette dictates that you be direct about your intentions but not act like an ass," he says. "It's no secret why you're there, so if you see a guy you'd like to spend some time with, you have to use the direct approach. Shy guys get no play at the baths, so you have to go up and ask him how he's doing." Make eye contact and get close so there's no mistaking your interest, but be sure not to corner him or yourself in case either of you decides to move off quickly. "Some guys are like Monet paintings," he explains. "They look beautiful from far off, but close up they're kind of splotchy messes." So Neil's not an art lover, but he's got a point. Bathhouses are usually pretty dimly lit. He continues, "If the guy you like walks off, it's okay. Don't stalk him. No one likes a shadow at these places. There are other guys there, so move on."

If a man you don't find attractive sidles up next to you, use the direct approach again and say, "No thanks," or, "I'm just looking." Voyeurism is an integral part of the bathhouse experience, so you won't be chastised for it. Don't be dismissive or rude, just direct.

In the darker rooms you'll have less opportunity to inspect the goods, so practicing safe sex is very important. Some baths have rules forbidding unsafe sex, but the rules aren't always enforced. Condoms are de rigueur for all anal sex at bathhouses (take a good look to be sure he's putting one on himself if you're the receptive partner), but not often for oral sex. If you prefer to suck with condoms you might consider not engaging in oral sex at all while at the baths.

You'll pass private rooms with doors open, and the guys inside will indicate by their posture what they're looking for, sexually speaking. A man on his stomach wants to get fucked. A man standing and stroking his dick wants to be sucked. If he's on his back stroking his cock, you'll have to ask him what he's looking for. If you encounter two or more guys playing together, wait until you're invited into the group before barging in. A nod or a "come here" finger gesture might be all you get, so you'd better be quick on the uptake.

Make sure to shower and wash thoroughly between encounters, and if you suspect your new partner hasn't properly washed up, just take him into the showers with you. He might like the friendly scrub down. Bathhouse customs vary from venue to venue and city to city, so watch, learn, play safe, and have fun.

NO. 80

How to Be the Hostess With the Mostest

So you're thinking of throwing a sex party or a jack-off party? A few pointers will keep the sexual energy high and keep your guests happy. First, you must clearly define for yourself what kind of event it will be.

Let's say you're planning a jack-off party where guys are just going to be stroking themselves and maybe each other, but not sucking or fucking. Make sure your guests know that. Some cities have institutionalized parties, often called "The Jacks" where the event is publicly advertised and an admission fee is charged. In those clubs, any penetration of any kind is grounds for people to be tossed out. If you're planning an at-home version of the same thing, let your guests know what activities will be allowed. Anyone who can't handle it shouldn't come.

A full-on orgy-style sex party is a different matter. Since guys will be doing anything and everything to each other all over, you'll need drop cloths or sheets over any furniture that could get soiled or stained by lube, and you'll need to provide condoms and lube (at floor level and in many locations) for easy access.

Vic, a 38-year-old executive in Marina Del Rey, California, and his friend Roman, a 40-year-old author from Venice Beach, throw a sex party every month or so, with anywhere from six to 25 men attending. Whoever hosts usually provides lube and condoms, and soda or cocktails, but many guys bring lube and condoms for themselves. Because the cost of the supplies can add up, sometimes they host the get-togethers in a hotel room instead and ask for donations from guys who attend, figuring in the cost of the room and the supplies into the requested contribution. "It's best to get a good mix of guys," says Vic. "There are a couple of total sluts that come every time, and it's great to have them there to ease in the newcomers. I make sure I only email the details on the location to the guys that are committed to showing up."

Vic stages the environment carefully, setting lights low but not dark and choosing music to set the mood. He knows that clubby house music can kill the mood when the diva starts wailing. "Trance or world beat music usually works best and not too loud. I'd rather hear the sounds of sex."

Since Vic's and Roman's guests are familiar with the routine, they know not to overaccessorize, and they behave well with new members. For first-time hosts, be sure you stay sober so you can monitor the proceedings (especially if it's in your house) and make sure everyone behaves in a gentlemanly manner. Roman says, "Even with the sex pigs, I make sure everyone is up-front about their HIV status, and anyone who isn't doesn't get invited back."

"Usually, guys take off their clothes as soon as they get inside," says Vic. "That way I know that there will be no wallflowers—at least no clothed wallflowers. If I know there are going to be a lot of guys, I get plastic sacks for the guys to put their clothes in."

And what about guys who like to kiss and tell? "What happens between us is supposed to stay within these walls. I'm not embarrassed about it, but I never tell anyone else who the guys are, or what they did when they were here. Some are married [to women] and some have boyfriends, so it's 'don't ask, don't tell.'"

CHAPTER 9

Role-play, Fantasy, and Advanced Study

★★

NO. 81

Play Kinky, But Not Like You Think

Your fantasy scenarios are your own— no one else's fantasies are going to be exactly like yours. Plenty of gay guys fantasize about Brad Pitt and his six-pack abs, but some guys prefer the mental image of pretty Brad gagged and strapped into a red patent-leather corset. *Vive la différence!* Some of your fantasies are going to be variations on a theme, but they're still not going to be exactly like mine, or exactly like those of the last guy you bonked, or like the kinks favored by the next guy you play with. A healthy fantasy life is the clean-burning fuel for your hybrid libido. It's what gets those juices going.

Close your eyes (not yet—do it after you read this paragraph) and picture your steamiest sexually charged fantasy. It could be the memory of some fantastic, torrid, and orgasmic moment where the sexual tension was so high you practically ripped your clothes off, or the moment where your entire body screamed for sex. Or picture a scenario you've imagined but never tried—the fantasy you've never told anyone about. Conjure that shadowy scene where the sounds, textures, and smells of sex surround you, where you're nervous but excited, where you know what you want but it's just out of reach. Or picture that encounter with the unexpected, when your anxiety, fear, or expectation made your stomach sink and your dick throb. Got it? Now grab your dick while you're thinking about it. Need a private moment? I'll wait.

Welcome back. Now that we've all had a mental escapade, think about the elements of your sizzling fantasy or sweltering memory. If it's a memory you conjured, think about what it was that made that time so spectacular. If you imagined a fantasy scene, what are the elements that make it so magnificent? The location? Your fantasy playmate? The mood? Props? Clothes? Sounds? The answers to these questions are the tools to turn your scenario into really fun sex play.

How do we turn the elements of our fantasy lives into real-life experiences? Most of us have some fantasies we haven't yet realized, stuff we'd want to try once, maybe more. When it comes to dressing up, getting tied down, or trying a little power play—let's call all that stuff "kink"—the good news is that kink, fantasy play, role-playing, and even BDSM (bondage/discipline, dominance/submission, sadomasochism) aren't as freaky or as uncommon as you might guess. If you've dreamed about it, chances are there's at least part of your kinky fantasy you can fulfill with a like-minded partner.

You don't have to own a full-body latex suit or even a simple riding crop to get into the action. Kink lite—some leather attire, a nipple clamp or two, calling him "Sir"—is pretty easy to get into. But heavy-duty kink—bondage, S/M, humiliation—requires a little thought and planning before you start. Kink is about exploring your sexual limits, so if you're interested in getting into a heavy-duty kink scene, you should spend some time thinking about why you haven't already done the things you fantasize about. If your answers include an aversion to pain (either giving or receiving it), emotional damage, concerns about the physical limits of your body, or genuine fear, then you might consider keeping those fantasies confined to your active internal life. Probably best not play them out in real life.

If, on the other hand, you always wanted to dress up like a sailor on shore leave and pretend as though you're cruising for rough play—and you haven't indulged your fantasy because you're ashamed of the idea or you're too straitlaced to try—then you should consider challenging yourself. If your fantasy doesn't hurt anyone else—physically or emotionally—and it won't hurt you, why not give it a go? If you decide that it doesn't work in real life like it did in your head, then draw another fantasy from the well of kink. It never runs dry.

NO. 82

Get Into S/M

So you want him to spank you, huh? To pin you down and make you beg for him to mistreat you? Perv.

Being the "bottom" in an S/M scene is a common fantasy. In fact, being the bottom (taking the submissive role) is usually the best place to start. It's the top (the dominant one) who sets up the scenario and controls what happens to whom and when—usually spanking, flogging, restraints, dripping wax, and the like. There's a certain ritualistic aspect to a lot of S/M play, so the best tops often begin as bottoms and learn the subtleties of power, control, and the human body's threshold for pain.

A good way to meet S/M tops is through a mutual acquaintance or in an event or venue sponsored by the leather community. Because of the vulnerability of the bottom in an S/M scene, meeting someone in a community is a wiser strategy than meeting a stranger over the Internet. The key word here is "community." A fully engaged member of a leather community is less likely to cause a novice bottom harm, or to take a scene further than the bottom really wants to go. No one wants a bad rep—it makes getting a date difficult.

Before getting into any S/M scenario, discuss your limits. Negotiating the scene is crucial to everyone's enjoyment and safety. While rape and abuse are often depicted in fantasy scenarios, they are just that: fantasies. Even if you're playing "rape," you have to set your boundaries before playtime. This negotiation will allow you both to trust each other, relax, and enjoy the scene. Just be honest about your wishes and your limits, and if your partner is into a kind of play that you've never tried but want to, tell him so and ease into that kind of play gently. If your prospective playmate won't talk openly about his limits and his familiarity with S/M before the scene begins, he's not the man/boy or master/slave for you.

In any kind of play where you're tempted to say "no!" as part of the scene (especially in role-play), make sure you have a safe word, a word (or a clearly visible action if one person is gagged) that is clearly understood by both parties to mean "Stop now and release/untie me!" Pick a word you wouldn't use as part of your scene (like "sassafras" or "succotash"), and make sure you are both comfortable using it when you feel real pain or need to stop the play for any reason.

For the eager beaver, there are specialty shops that cater to kinky sex play. You can get harnesses, chaps, hats, cats-o'-nine-tails, shackles, stretchers (bars that keep hands or legs forced apart), and instruction books for specialized play. Start small and, if you like it, add to your kink collection.

This isn't like joining a cult or buying a Saturn. Your experimentation with kink need not be a whole lifestyle if you don't want to make it one. You don't have to get an entire dungeon in order to smack his ass with a studded paddle; you just have to make sure he wants to have his ass paddled. If you're not interested in joining a whole community to work out your kinks, just take the BDSM elements you're interested in, and dive in. Again, just communicate with your partner about the play before the scene actually starts. Have a few chats about it, send each other dirty e-mail missives with do-and-don't lists, or leave explicit Post-its in each other's wallets. The point is to maintain the impulsiveness of the scene *and* lay out your ground rules. Consent and spontaneity are not mutually exclusive. The more you get to know each other's likes and dislikes, the easier it will be to slip into the kink mode spontaneously.

NO. 83 Exhibitionism/Voyeurism Scenario: Pizza Delivery

Let's extrapolate from a bit of junior high school terminology: If first base is making out, second base is rubbing the fun bits under the clothes, third base is making out with clothes off, and a home run is oral and/or anal sex, then role-play is a whole bunch of fun stuff you can do in the dugout before you're up to bat. Or even after you've hit a homer.

By my count, an admittedly unscientific one, there are four basic categories of role-play scenarios: (1) exhibitionism and voyeurism, (2) power sex, (3) resistance sex, and (4) the forbidden. Below we'll go over some examples of each kind of play and sketch out a scenario that you can set up at home.

Let's start with a little exhibitionism and voyeurism, shall we? There are dozens of role-play scenes that could fall under this category, where the most important elements are your body and his eyes, or vice versa. Does it turn you on to watch someone getting undressed, masturbating, or playing with sex toys? Does it get you hot to see someone who knows he's being watched? Do you get off putting on a show for a guy?

College guys in a dorm together get horny, and chances are one of them is going to start slapping his meat around sooner or later. Your roommate might be shy about it, or he might do it in the bed next to yours when he knows you can hear him. Your next-door neighbor is a cutie, and you'd love to see him naked. One day you notice he's been leaving his blinds open at night so that you can see right into this bedroom. He seems to know you're watching, and he likes to flex and pose for you.

For this example of exhibition and voyeurism, let's illuminate an old porno trope: "Pizza Deliveryman and Customer."

Player #1: Horny Pizza Delivery Guy
What's my motivation? You're horny and you deliver pizza.

Player #2: Horny Customer
What's my motivation? You're hungry but also horny. You're not sure where your wallet is.

Set the scene: This works best in the evening. The pizza man goes outside and waits for a few minutes. The customer stays inside, wearing a bathrobe, or just shorts, or anything that slips open or off easily. Pizza man should find a window to look through and watch for a minute or two before knocking on the door, pizza in hand.

Tools of the trade: Pizza, door, window

Sample dialogue to get you started:
Pizza Man: Hello, sir. Large pizza with extra anchovies. That'll be $15.

Customer: Come in. My goodness, you're so (*take your pick:* tall, cute, built, handsome). You're not the regular delivery guy.

Pizza Man: Right. That's my cousin Vinnie. He's in jail, so I'm filling in for him. Just extra anchovies, huh? You don't like sausage?

Customer: Oh, I like sausage all right. Hang on a minute while I get my wallet. [*Looks around for wallet but can't seem to find it. Robe slips open a little bit, or his cock slips out the front flap of his boxers, but he pretends not to notice. Gets money and gives it to pizza guy while standing really close.*]

Pizza Man: I like sausage too. [*Rubs crotch so that Customer can see. Looks him right in the eye. Takes money, moves to the door.*]

Customer: Thanks, man. Have a good night.

[*Door closes behind him. Customer takes pizza and sits down. Pizza Man stays close to a window where he can see the Customer slide off his shorts and start to eat the pizza naked. Pizza man is outside, getting hard watching. Customer notices the face peering in the window and decides to stand up and walk around naked, flex his muscles, stroke his dick, anything that gets him hot to know someone else is watching...*]

No. 84

Power Scenario: Meter Man

Power play is the basis for much of S/M play. It's a situation in which one man yields control to another man. Why give up power? Yielding control can be incredibly erotic.

The master/slave setup is a common one, but if that seems a little too hard-core for you, think of another situation in which you'd be willing to give up total control to another person. Invention is the mother of good sex play, so get creative. Authority figures also work well here.

Let's say you're walking back to your car and you see a parking-meter guy writing you a ticket for an expired meter. He doesn't know it, but your glove compartment is full of unpaid parking tickets, and getting another one will surely mean your car will be impounded. You might even go to jail. We'll call this scene "The Meter Man."

Player #1: Horny Motorist
What's my motivation? Too many parking tickets means a jail sentence. Go with the flow here...it's theatrical, remember? You'll do anything—and you mean *anything*—to avoid this ticket. Plus, authority and uniforms make you hot.

Player #2: Horny Meter Man
What's my motivation? It's the job of a civil servant to maintain order in this society, and parking tickets are your contribution to that order. But civil servants have needs too.

Set the scene: Start outside on a quiet street, away from other people and traffic. The meter man should be writing out a ticket on his notepad.

Tools of the trade: Motorist should have a car and a penchant for getting punished for his bad parking. The meter man should have a goofy meter-man hat, drab color- less uniform, notepad, pen, rigid authoritarian attitude, avi- ator glasses (they work in almost any role-play scene).

Sample dialogue to get you started:

Motorist: [*Runs up to car.*] Wait, don't write that ticket! I was just about to (*pick one:* put coins in the meter, pull off the curb, drive away from the fire hydrant).

Meter Man: Oh, that's a shame. Look, I've already writ- ten it. [*Rips ticket off pad and puts under windshield wiper.*]

Motorist: No! No way, you can't ticket me! I've already got 18 unpaid parking tickets, and this one means I could be going to jail. I can't go to jail!

Meter Man: Look, pal, you screwed up and you're going to have to pay for it. Poor parking is the downfall of our cul- ture. It's another loose chink in the armor of civilization. If I let you park (in front of a fire hydrant, without feeding the meter, at this bike rack), what's next?

Motorist: Man, this is awful. I'd do almost anything to get out of this ticket. Isn't there anything we can compromise on? [*Touches meter man's chest.*]

Meter Man: This is definitely a punishable offense. You deserve far worse than jail.

Motorist: Oh, I agree. But wouldn't you rather punish me yourself?

NO. 85 Resistance Scenario: Corrupt General and Rebel Leader

A resistance scenario is a form of power play with a twist. It's not a simple power game where one man decides what happens to the other man. Resistance play involves more of a contest of wills. Think of games where the winner gets to decide what happens to the loser—whether he sucks the winner's dick, whether the winner fucks him, or whether he has to fuck the winner. Resistance play can be more of a mind-fuck—and therefore very exciting! Wrestling is a common form of resistance play. There are plenty of others.

For this example, we'll use a prison guard and a prisoner. To make the scenario a little more exotic (and theatrical), I drew inspiration from the 1985 movie *Kiss of the Spider Woman*. Feel free to substitute your Latin American dictator captors with Nazis, Fascists, Republicans, the FCC, or whomever you please.

Player #1: Horny Corrupt General (heavy Central American accent optional)
What's my motivation? You live to torture and humiliate

your political prisoners. One prisoner in particular has a really nice ass, which turns you on.

Player #2: Horny Political Prisoner
What's my motivation? You are a rebel for the cause of independence, and you'd rather die than be subjected to the humiliation of your (hot) prison guard.

Set the Scene: Any dingy, cramped room will stand in for a jail cell: a basement, a laundry room, or a garage. The prisoner should be restrained with shackles or rope against a wall.

Tools of the trade: Shackles are great, but padded leather wrist restraints will work as well. The general should be dressed in khaki or army greens and wear a Fidel-style hat (bonus: they're in style now too). The prisoner should wear smudged, torn clothes, as though he's been savagely beaten by corrupt police. The guard might smoke a cigar and wear aviator glasses; those are nice porny touches. A riding crop is a nice touch.

Sample dialogue to get you started:

General: [*Enters cell, wielding riding crop.*] Get up, scum. It's time for inspection.

Prisoner: I will never obey you or your corrupt regime, you fascist pig! [*Spits at the feet of his captor.*]

General: Get up now or you'll wish you had obeyed. [*Smacks prisoner with riding crop.*] We have your (mother, favorite pet, boyfriend, little sister) in a detention cell not far from here. (He/she/it) is in a very delicate condition. You wouldn't want to jeopardize (his/her/its) health any further, would you? [*Prisoner stands up grudgingly.*] Very good. Turn around so I may assess your condition. [*Prisoner turns around. General rips shirt off prisoner and pulls pants down so that clothes hang in rags off his body.*]

Prisoner: You son of a bitch! You may destroy my body, but you'll never take my spirit!

General: I wouldn't dare destroy such a beautiful body. [*General strokes prisoner's torso or ass with the riding crop.*]

Prisoner: Do your worst. I will never comply!

NO. 86 Forbidden Scenario: Priest and Parishioner

Forbidden sex play takes the thrill of taboo and turns it into kink. There are people who we're told are off-limits for sex: Family members aren't supposed to do it with each other, teachers aren't supposed to do it with students, coaches aren't supposed to do it with the players, and priests and monks aren't supposed to do it with anyone. (Apologies to the religious readers here! This is not an indictment of organized religion, priests, or ardent believers. It's a sex book, for crying out loud!)

Imagine a teacher keeping a student after class as punishment for mouthing off, or a coach forcing a sweaty football player to do push-ups in the locker room. Picture monks in itchy robes who have taken vows of silence and who have been cooped up in a monastery for years without being able to satisfy their carnal urges. And what about "The Priest and Parishioner"?

Player #1: Horny Priest
What's my motivation? You're interested in the will of God and all that, but that robe is hot and heavy, and you wouldn't mind scratching the occasional impure itch.

Player #2: Horny Parishioner
What's my motivation? It's tough to be a pious virgin when you fantasize about sex with hot guys. You feel the need to get your mortal transgressions off your chest.

Set the Scene: Any screen or curtain can work as the wall of a confessional booth. Dim the lights and light some candles. You can play religious music, like Gregorian chant, or quasi-religious music if it has a sexual undertone, like Enigma.

Tools of the trade: The Priest should wear a robe (with little or nothing underneath) and carry a rosary.

Sample dialogue to get you started:

Parishioner: Forgive me, Father, for I have sinned. It has been eight years my last confession. These are my sins. I have masturbated three times a day since I was 14. I have purchased dirty magazines. I have had impure thoughts. I have lusted after my neighbor.

Priest: Well, son, that's not so bad. It's all pretty normal for a young man your age. Tell me about it.

Parishioner: Well, he's tall, dark—

Priest: *He?* Are you a homosexual, son?

Parishioner: Well, I don't know. I've never had sex with another person.

Priest: Well, tell me what you fantasize about when you think about sex. Do you always think about men? Tell me what you imagine them doing to you. [*Priest should take out cock and start masturbating while parishioner talks.*]

Parishioner: Father, I'm not sure I feel comfortable with doing this in the confessional. Maybe if we could talk face-to-face.

NO. 87 Tan That Hide

Who doesn't love a good, loud, smack on the ass? Whether you prefer the satisfying and perfect *thwap!* when your hand meets a ripe, round ass cheek, or the little tingle your tush gives off for some time afterward, spanking is fun, animalistic, and totally sexy.

Spanking can be a great part of S/M or role-playing (scenes of frat hazing and parochial-school punishment come to mind), or it can be just a fantastic way to turn up the volume to eleven when you're already in the throes of piggy sex. Yes, your ass will get red and sore, but pain can be a good thing. During arousal, your blood pressure goes up, your heart rate goes up, and your breathing quickens—all of which helps turn sensations you might otherwise interpret as pain (nibbles, bites, spanking, getting fucked) into pleasure. Releasing endorphins and adrenaline is your body's way of handling stress and pain, and they induce a natural high as well. Deep breathing and relaxation—along with some well-timed yelps, if you feel moved to squeal—will help you endure more pain (assuming you want to endure more pain) when you're getting your ass smacked.

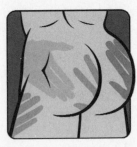

If you're going to lay your hands on each other, keep a couple of things in mind. First, you've got to smack him like you mean it. A limp-wristed, halfhearted thunk won't get anyone's juices flowing. Each ass is shaped differently and has different acoustic qualities, so smack all over until you get the sound you like, being careful not to smack the crack—the vibrations can rattle balls unpleasantly. Stay away from the spine and tailbone, and focus on the fleshy parts. Warm up the ass with some medium-strength smacks and build up the pressure and frequency. Dishing out a thunderous ass attack right off the bat will cut your spank sesh short.

Your body's responses, combined with the memory of the sound that slap makes, will turn the little purple finger-shaped welts you'll get the next morning into friendly souvenirs of a good time.

NO. 88 Quick and Easy Bondage

Bondage runs the gamut—tying his wrists to the bedpost with your least-favorite necktie, putting him in handcuffs, or tying him up in a series of Japanese bondage knots that would give any sailor a headache.

You don't have to go right for the iron shackles and hang upside down over the East River, Houdini-style. Simple restraints, even ones that can be undone in a pinch if the situation demands, can fulfill the psychological need to be tied up. It's no wonder that type-A personalities—the go-getter guys who are so in control of their day-to-day lives—are often the ones who get the most out of being the bottom in a bondage scene. They get off on surrendering control and taking whatever the top guy dishes out. It's also no wonder S/M and bondage scenes mesh well together. Bondage can mean yielding control or taking it, but which way the flow goes doesn't matter so long as each party is getting what he wants out of the scenario. Here are some basic tips for beginners:

★ Rope is clearly the tool of choice, but since it's going to be right against you skin, take care to select a material like cotton clothesline that won't abrade your sensitive epidermis (see Secret #69, dude!).

★ Get at least 100 feet of rope (no thinner than half an inch) so you can divide it into different lengths. Use shorter bits (a dozen feet or so) for tying up hands or feet, and the longer bits for more elaborate bondage.

★ If you can't get your hands on some rope, PVC tape will work because it sticks to itself, not to your skin. Sports tape works well too because it's designed not to irritate skin. Beware that tape traps body heat and can cause body temperature to rise. If you're going to use tape, make sure the room isn't too hot and that the guy getting taped up doesn't get too warm.

★ Silk scarves (not that you have any around the house) may look glam, but knots in silk can get too tight to untie.

★ Keep some scissors on hand in case you've got to cut each other loose in a hurry.

★ There are some techniques that should be considered totally off-limits for neophytes. Do not try electricity play, suspension from the ceiling or wall, mummification, or that crazy shit that guys in the Lollapalooza side shows used to do—suspending weights from body piercings, piercing the skin with needles (or anything else!), or branding.

★ Don't make any restraints too tight. Keep one or two finger widths between any restraint and the flesh, especially around the chest where breathing can be hampered, and around vital organs and joints. These are areas where blood flow can easily be restricted. Use square knots that can be undone quickly if need be.

★ Never leave a bound person alone for any length of time, especially if he is facedown or bound in a standing position. The risk of fainting, pinched nerves, or suffocation is simply too great.

★ If you want to make bondage a regular part of your sex play, or if you want to learn more complex bondage techniques, pick up a book like *The Seductive Art of Japanese Bondage* by Midori for more detailed information.

NO. 89 Outdoor Sex

Dan, 23, and Greg, 30, have a pretty wild sex life (one they freely discuss with their friends), and it's only gotten hotter since they started taking it outdoors. Says Dan: "Aside from the chance of getting caught—" ("A highly likely chance given some of our locations lately," Greg interrupts.) "Aside from that," Dan continues, "sex is totally different outside. The air smells different. There's a breeze, and even when it's not in a wooded or natural place—like if it's in a parking lot or someplace like that—it still feels more natural to have sex outside." Outdoor sex has become their favorite activity, and they go driving in search of outdoor sex spots once a week or so during warm weather. Luckily, they live in Phoenix, Arizona, where the weather is year-round warm.

"Plus, there are all the stars out, if you do it at night," adds Greg. "At the risk of sounding a little cosmic, it's a thrill to be on my back, having sex while looking up at Dan and the big sky and all the stars behind him."

And if someone approaches or walks by? "I like to imagine someone watching, and sometimes someone is, but we mostly just quiet down to see if it's a cop or a park ranger," says Dan. "And if it isn't, we just go back to the sex. They can get their jollies by watching if they like. It doesn't bother me."

Follow Dan and Greg's lead and take your favorite sport outside:

★ Chose locales that are inconspicuous and out of the way, and stick to nighttime romps. You're less likely to attract the attention of passers-by or the local constabulary. Think of it this way: The farther away you are from other people, the louder you can be.

★ Bring along that blanket that you stowed away in your car. The great outdoors are full of dirt, foliage, and rocks—none of which is likely to be as comfortable as your bed at home (or your kitchen floor, or the top of the washing machine). A blanket or sleeping bag is the next best thing.

★ Just because you're out in nature doesn't mean you can forgo the generous use of lube. Dig into your sex-to-go kit (Secret #71) and pull out those single-serving lube packets.

★ Be smart about the weather. If it's too cold to be bare-ass naked outside, it's probably too cold to do the chores outdoors. If it's too cold to fuck outside, try your car, or maybe just screw near a window where you can *look* outside.

★ Be sneaky. If you're headed into the woods, bring along a tent, some firewood, or other camping paraphernalia. Your fellow campers will never suspect your ulterior motive. Leave the collapsible sling at home.

★ If you want to screw on the strand, a quick jump in the ocean afterward will help get the sand out of your crevices. Many public beaches have shower facilities. Take a bathing suit along and put it on to rinse off.

★ Even if you have no plan to follow the laws of your state or city regarding sex in public (and they vary from place to place), you should know what the laws are. Punishments for public indecency can vary from fines to jail time. If you get caught, be mild-mannered and get dressed, but don't admit to a police officer that you were having sex, or doing anything illegal. Comply with the officer's requests to provide ID.

★ Two words: *insect repellent.* Eleven more words: *Keep the repellent off any body part you want to suck.*

Smile for the Camera
A homemade porno can be so much hotter than the mass-produced kind. I mean no disrespect to studio-generated

porn (okay, I mean *some* disrespect). You bet I'll still rent the newest skin flick DVDs, even though the current crop is mostly populated with dazed, overgrown, steroid-pitted models whose interaction with one another has had every shred of spontaneity and lust edited away. I yearn for the days of porn on real celluloid where production values and passion still mattered—or at least it looked like it mattered. Blame it on cheap digital technology if you like. Luckily, where cheaply procured modern technology has done porn a disservice, it's done the do-it-yourselfer a great service. The advent of the home video camera means that if we don't like the porn out there, we can make our own.

As with all sexual acts, videotaping your trysts demands the consent of all the people involved. Whether you want to tape a private lovemaking session with a long-time partner or a group grope with a gaggle of guys, you'd better make sure that anyone whose business gets captured on tape is cool with it.

Plenty of exhibitionists love the thought of being caught on tape in the throes of ecstasy. If "Lights, camera, action!" is a turn-on, then buy or borrow a camera and get to work. Here are some tips to make a good (and ethically sound) homemade porno.

★ Discuss who gets the finished tape or digital copy of the footage and how it's going to be used. Screenings with friends? Your personal Web page? Just be sure to clarify how you'll use the footage.

★ If you don't want the footage to be duplicated, you should be in charge of the format (if it's digital), or you should select a nondigital format like VHS that enables you to actually *see* the tape and take it with you when your acting debut has ended.

★ Get the consent of everyone involved. If more than just you and your partner are involved, have each individual on the footage give his consent. He can give consent either by looking into the camera and saying so, or by signing a note that indicates he knows he's being taped and how the tape will be used. It may sound clinical, but you don't want your ass to get sued, as was the case for Paris Hilton or R. Kelley.

★ Speaking of R. Kelley: For crying out loud, don't do anything illegal on tape, if you ever plan to show it to anyone else. That means no drugs and no sex with minors (and not just on videotape—*never*); no sex with unconscious people (again, *never!*); no sex with animals; and no violence—even if your partner agrees to it. R. Kelley got caught. Rob Lowe got caught. Don't risk it.

★ Lighting is key. Unless you've got an infrared attachment for your lens, keep a few lights on so you can see the lip-smackin' ass-slappin' action. It's not much of a turn-on, if you pop the finished tape into the VCR and all you can see are the whites of your eyes and teeth. Do a little video test first.

★ Get a tripod and use it.

★ Make a test video of a little bit of solo stroking action—to test the camera's angle and zoom, the lighting, and the sound. Make the frame sufficiently wide to capture activity on the sides of the bed or while you're kneeling or standing in the bed, but not so far back that you need a big-screen TV to see the action in replay.

★ Clothes make the man. But slowly removing some sexy clothes on tape makes the man horny.

CHAPTER 10

Romance, Passion, and Leaving a Lasting Impression

★★

NO. 91

Why Romance?

What's romance got to do with a book for gay guys? Gay men are only interested in sex and stuff that can get them into the sack, right? This book is called *101 Gay Sex Secrets Revealed*, not *101 Romantic Clichéd Girly Things You Can Do Instead of Fucking*, right?

To you barbarians out there, I have two things to say to that. Number One: The big secret here is that many guys love to be romanced. It's not just a girly thing. Some guys—including some who have the heaviest homo-kink hardware stashed under their beds and some who talk dirty, like truck drivers on crystal meth—actually like to cuddle by candlelight, or watch the sunset while holding hands, or whisper sweet nothings into their boyfriends' ears. Hot sex and romance aren't mutually exclusive. Your dick can get hard, and your heart can flutter for the same guy—sometimes even at the same time. Number Two: Even if you are really only interested in sex and find relationships as appealing as paper cuts on your tongue, you better learn how to pour on the romance, buddy. Some guys only like to get sixty-nined after they've been wined and dined.

Why does romance work for some guys? Think about a time you've been treated like a king, a time when the guy you were with was so thoughtful and so caring that you were literally swooning. Wouldn't you have done almost anything in bed that he wanted you to do? If you haven't had such luck, then imagine yourself as Julia Roberts in *Pretty Woman*. When Richard Gere climbed out of the roof of that limo with flowers in his teeth, looking like a knight in shining Armani, wouldn't you just have dropped to your knees right there on that fire escape and given him the best blow job he'd ever had? My point exactly. Romance can stoke the embers of passion.

Lee, 35, says that Dallas, 40, a man he met in an online gay chat room, is one of the best sexual partners he's ever had. After they exchanged nude pictures of themselves and some provocative instant messages, they met for sex and had a great time. After that meeting, they made another date, then another. While the two still aren't exactly boyfriends, Lee says, "Dallas has the ability to make me feel like he wants me so bad it's eating him up inside. It's a total thrill. He always sets a mood with low lighting and sometimes candles. He puts on some great music, something low and sexy, and he always looks me in the eye and says my name while we're having sex. Afterward, he always jumps in the shower with me, and he soaps my body from head to toe—he even washes my hair. It's a totally romantic experience. He is so attentive. Now I can practically come just hearing his voice."

Romance is about making your partner feel that he's exactly what you want, what you need, and what you must have. When your partner is taking pains to focus all his attention on you, it's easy to feel like you're the only man in the world for him—rather than the only guy in the room at that particular moment. And desire is the most potent aphrodisiac. When a man really wants you, when you can see it in his eyes (and not just in the tenting crotch of his pants), it can send your internal sex-o-meter through the roof. Act like he's the only one in the world for you, and he'll respond the same way.

NO. 92 (Don't) Get a Room!

Public displays of affection are incredibly effective bonding activities. Not only does two men holding hands indicate affection from one man to the other, it also sends an important public message.

Public displays of affection are significant for more than just the two guys involved. Take the simplest form of public affection: holding hands. When you hold his hand, you indicate this to anyone who can see you: "Yes, we're gay! Yes, we like each other! No, how we show our affection is not subject to your approval!"

Why is taking his hand so exciting? Aside from the fact that the hands are often woefully neglected as erogenous zones during sex, they are often the first part of his body you'll touch when you meet—a handshake. Whether you're holding his hand or putting your hand on his shoulder (or his thigh), the first touch (assuming you didn't meet in a bathhouse or by literally bumping into each other at a circuit party when you were already nearly naked) can be positively electrifying.

The difference between the acceptance of gay displays of affection now versus several decades ago is enormous. The shock of seeing men holding hands or kissing when they greet one another has largely subsided, at least in major metropolitan areas, so grab his hand! Kiss his cheek! Wrap your arm around his waist!

Such displays, like gay images on TV and in film, are vitally important. They are the gestures that slowly chip away at polite homophobia—the "I'm not a bigot, but why can't they stay quiet and out of sight"—brand of homophobia practiced by so many people. Cultural attitudes can and do change, and you can be an agent of that change. Be an activist! Kiss him in a crowded plaza or hold his hand as you're leaving an airplane. Your sex life—and your world—will only get better.

NO. 93 A Little Bit of Mystery

What made James Bond such an object of desire? (Think early Sean Connery, not late Roger Moore.) Why is the idea of a spy or a CIA agent so seductive? It's the allure of the unknown, the secretive, the hint that behind his eyes there's an internal dialogue going on, to which you don't have access. In other words, he's a little bit of mystery.

Mystery, for better or for worse, is a powerful part of attraction. Mystery is a double-edged sword—he may just be shy, or maybe he's on the run from the feds. But it's the very suggestion of danger that makes even a little mystery so tantalizing. Spice up a first date or a longtime relationship with a little dash of mystery or the occasional surprise.

Reserving some information about yourself when you're getting to know a guy gives you an instant allure, a cachet that will draw him to you, making him want more. While they can't be accused of dishonesty, men whose lives are open books hardly make for exciting first dates. If he hands you his résumé, his head shot, or his book (God, no!), you're not quite as likely to feel the draw of the unknown. So don't spill your guts when you meet a new guy. He doesn't need to know you have acid reflux disease or an incontinent cocker spaniel. He can learn that stuff at a more leisurely pace.

Jean-Pierre, 30, a DJ in Chicago, plays a little game on first dates. "At the very beginning of the date, I say that I'm going to tell him one lie sometime during the evening and that I won't tell him what the lie is until I see him the next time. If he likes the idea of the game, I'll tell him to do the same thing for me. It really keeps him on his toes and keeps him interested in what I'm saying that night." A little caveat to Jean-Pierre's suggestion: Keep the lie to one, please.

Another technique for keeping your date on his toes comes from Joseph, 28, a filmmaker who lives in Los

Angeles. He and his boyfriend of five years, Franco, 33, like to go out dancing at gay clubs. "One time when we were on a vacation in Brazil," says Joseph, "we were at this big club, and tons of beautiful men were all around us. I was standing right behind Franco near the dance floor—in plain sight of all these men—and I unzipped my fly and pulled his hand back behind him and slid it into my pants. I was wearing a cock ring, and my dick was hard. He didn't know I was wearing it, and he was a little surprised. It was the little secret we shared—him feeling my dick in this public place and him knowing that I was wearing a cock ring—and it really got him going. He built up a lot of sexual energy that I helped him release later that night."

NO. 94

Know What Not to Say

Openness and honesty are vital, especially in a new relationship. But there's a customary learning curve that goes along with dating a new guy, especially during the first few months. At first, you often know nothing about a new date except for what he looked like covered in sweat on a dance floor, what his online dating profile said, or the book he was reading when you said hi at the coffee shop. Those first few months are crucial because they're the time you can learn the most about a steady date or potential partner. The learning curve is steep, and saying the wrong thing at the wrong time can throw you right off that steep curve.

The first year of dating moves through distinct phases,

and an inappropriate or overly intimate statement can turn off a gay man in a new relationship faster than mismatched patterns or the image of Janet Reno in a tube top. Knowing how to negotiate that learning curve can enable you to have a much more successful dating career.

Phase I—the first two weeks (or up to three dates): Aside from your personal laundry list of things that draw you to a new beau (Is he a smoker? Does he have a job? Does he like German Expressionist cinema?), at this stage you should address two main concerns. The first is finding out whether your date is a garden-variety psycho. Ask about his mom, his job, whether he's been to prison, etc. The second issue is sexual attraction. Does he appeal to you enough to take him home? You don't have to fuck around with him in the first two weeks if you don't play that way, but at the very least you should probably *want* to. If he's not an ax-murderer and you want to see him naked and moaning your name, you'll probably get past these two weeks with flying colors. Just make sure you don't come off as a psycho either.

Things not to say to him during Phase I:

★ "Sure, what the hell, I can have a cocktail with you. What do those 'doctors' really know about reactions to antipsychotic meds anyway?"

★ "If I could just get that felony conviction overturned, I could get a decent job."

★ "Could you excuse me for a moment? I just need a good cry right now."

★ "I love you."

Phase II—the first two months: In this stage, you'll discover a bit more about your beau's life—who his friends are, what his work is about, and what he likes to do when he's got some downtime. The sex is very exciting in this stage, since you'll get to know each other's proclivities.

Things not to say during Phase II:
★ "You remind me of my mother. Maybe this relationship will turn out better."
★ "All my previous relationships have ended badly. They all dumped me. And there have been a *lot*."
★ "I hate my boss. I totally understand how those postal employees with semiautomatic weapons felt."
★ "I love you."

Phase III—up to six months: This stage is about exploring your relationship together, spending more nights at each other's places, and maybe taking the occasional weekend getaway together. You still don't fart in front of each other (often), but you can get more relaxed. The possibility of commitment may come up. Don't jump the gun.

Things not to say during Phase III:
★ "I need to borrow some money. Okay, a lot of money. And in small, unmarked bills."
★ "How soon is too soon to move in together?"
★ "It's not really cheating if the other guy know about it, right?"
★ "I love you."

Save the *I love you*s for after the first six months at the earliest, and don't consider moving in together until after the first year of dating. True, these are just rules of thumb, but before you make a big decision like shacking up you'll want to spend a full year in his life. Consider him probationary in the meantime. Holidays are particularly telling. Pay close attention to what happens when tax day rolls around (how does he handle money?), during Thanksgiving, Christmas, or Hanukkah (how does he relate to his family?), Easter (is he headed to the White Party? If so, are you too?), Summer Solstice (does he dress up like a satyr and howl at the moon?), and other holidays. How he handles each of these red-letter dates will tell you volumes about his personality.

Field Trip: The Grocery Store

You don't need to see *9 1/2 Weeks* to imagine what it must be like to smear a naked lover with all manner of food and then eat it off his body. Sex and food often go together well, on-screen or off. You've heard that eating chocolate releases the same mood-elevating brain chemicals that being in love does, right? Try drizzling chocolate on his cock and then licking if off. You'll love that too, and you'll be releasing helpful brain chemicals left and right.

If your flights of fancy tend toward the culinary, then grab your buddy and make a trip to the local grocery store to shop together for some items to coat each other with. You don't really even have to be all that excited about the act of smearing each other with food—a shopping trip with a salacious agenda can be titillating all by itself. While you're walking down the frozen-food aisle, lean close and tell him, "I want to lick marshmallow paste off your ass cheeks." Grocery shopping suddenly becomes more appealing. (Just remember that many foods are incompatible with latex condoms; try polyurethane.)

The most common sex foods are those found in the dessert aisle. The aforementioned chocolate sauce and the familiar whipped cream (the kind in the pressurized can) are old standbys for a reason—they're fun to drizzle or spritz into a lover's hills and valleys. But beware: They are full of sugar, so his skin will be sticky after your feast. That can be a bonus if you like sticky and messy. It can also be an occasion to hop into the shower together.

Champagne is good on the surface of the skin (the effervescence is nice), but it tends to dry out the mucous membranes, so don't try it in lieu of lube. Ice cubes are also an old standby; the freezing sensation makes for some seriously hard nipples and can lead to some well-orchestrated chills, plus there's no residue and only a little puddle to clean up. You planned on cleaning up a puddle of another kind anyway, right?

The flavor of foods can be used to mask the natural musk of the male body—if you're not a fan of certain musky scents. Say your boyfriend wants you to eat out his freshly showered ass, but despite assurances that he's spic-and-span, the thought turns you off. A little marmalade or Jell-O on his pretty little pucker might make your first tongue trip up his alley a little more inviting.

Stay away from any hot or spicy foods flavored with peppers or chiles. The active ingredient in chilies and hot peppers is capsaicin, a chemical compound that's really, really unfriendly to your mucous membranes, eyes, nostrils, dick, and butthole. Even when you steer clear of the most sensitive parts, chile oils have a tendency to get on your hands, then transfer to any parts you touch. Yelling "It burns!" is rarely a turn-on. So skip the curry and the salsa.

M&M's, pudding, ice cream, escargot, oyster crackers—whatever you pick to dip into, dribble on, or lick off your lover—just experiment with different textures and tastes. No need to tuck a napkin anywhere. *Bon appétit!*

No. 96 Role-Play—Fully Dressed and in Public

We know role-play works in the bedroom. We know it's a good way to get into the mood, spice up your nude playtime, and up the stakes, sexually speaking. Setting the mood can work outside the boudoir as well. Why not take the opportunity for you and your partner to be someone other than yourselves for a night?

Dean and Boyd, who are 28 and 32 respectively, met at a cocktail party in Los Angeles in June. Then Dean, an actor, had to leave town to go on location for a film shoot until August. The two were smitten almost immediately, so they continued a courtship over the phone while Dean was away. Says Boyd: "I was so excited for him to come back, so in the last week before he returned, I told him that it would be fun if we didn't meet up right away but went to the same bar and pretended to pick each other up. We met at the bar, and I said hi. I got to ask him what he does for a living—he said he was a flight attendant, so I said, 'What a coincidence. I'm writing an article on flight attendants.' It was goofy stuff, but the cruising was so much fun—him touching me in a really flirty way, like he didn't know me well but was hitting on me. We went home together after an hour or so, totally pawing each other. We could hardly get inside my apartment with all our clothes on!"

Anderson, 26, and Wyatt, 25, like their role-play a little different. They prefer to pretend to fight like cats and dogs, often in crowded places in Brooklyn. "We get a weird charge out of play fighting," says Wyatt. "We'll be on the train together, and no one will be talking, then out of the blue he'll tell me how much he hates my cologne, and I'll say 'You bought it for me, asshole!' Then he'll say he gave it to me because it was the cheapest he could find. Pretty soon we're fighting and talking over each other, like the couple on *Moonlighting,* and everyone around us is a little shocked. Then we'll suddenly start making out or something. People have no idea what we're up to. It's great and it gets me worked up." Drama queens! But hey, it works for them.

No. 97 Get Sweaty Together

Bars, clubs, restaurants, and movie theaters aren't the only places to enjoy time with a date. Besides the fact that those places aren't always favorable to conversation, and they can be costly ($16 martinis?!) and uncomfortable for get-to-know-you dates.

Gay places like bars and clubs often have a competitive

air that can hinder your concentrating on each other. You don't want him looking over your shoulder at other guys when you're asking him about his political views, and if he's shy, you don't want to bump into 30 of your closest friends and ex-boyfriends while you're on your date.

Try getting physical together by taking an evening hike, playing tennis or racquetball, in-line skating, swimming at the beach—anything that will get you sweating and your blood pumping. Sweating with someone is a great way to build a connection with him, and regular activity (aside from forearm and jaw exercises in the steam room at your health club) is healthy.

You needn't be an athlete to go bowling or take a moonlight walk. But taking a bike ride (they're available for rent, if you don't have your own) or signing up for a little competitive physical activity can spark the kind of playful interaction that leads to lines like, "If you win, you can do anything you like to me in bed."

NO. 98 Get Dirty Together

The kind of passion that unhinges you is every bit as memorable as romantic gestures like flowers and chocolates. Flowers wilt. Chocolate is loaded with calories. But hot, nasty sex lasts a lifetime. Sometimes being dirty with a willing coconspirator in an unexpected place can create a memory that you can giggle about for years to come, and it's good imagination fodder for an alone-time session. Discreet sex in an otherwise sexless environment can turn a dull social event or standard shopping trip into a thrilling tryst. Most any old place will work—a dinner party, a theme park, your old bedroom in your parents' house, and especially any place with a locking door. Just be sure no one can walk in you—at least no one who isn't interested in seeing you getting down.

Tomas, 27, a software engineer in Charlotte, North Carolina, recalls a time when a dull work reception turned into an exciting evening. "We had this engineering conference to go to, and afterward the company threw a cocktail reception that my boss expected me to attend. I invited my then-boyfriend, John, and after an hour or so of standing around bored in this hotel bar, John and I slipped off to the bathroom and locked a stall door, and I gave John a quickie blow job. We went back to the party, and then later on we slipped off again and he sucked me off. It made all the business chitchat in between tolerable, and now I drop into that bar occasionally for a drink just to remind myself of how fun it was."

Taking a cue from tearoom cruising, Paul, 40, an artist in Washington, D.C., occasionally takes a break from shopping with his boyfriend to slip into the bathroom in a large department store or the dressing room in a boutique clothing shop for a quickie: "You have to be careful because big department stores sometimes won't let you into the dressing rooms with another person, but if it's really busy or really slow, they won't notice the two sets of legs under the door."

Get Jealous Occasionally

So you've been seeing some guy for a while. Maybe you've said the *c* word ("commitment") or the *m* word ("monogamy"). Or maybe you haven't yet, but things are still going swimmingly. You and your man gaze lovingly at each other. He's okay, and you're okay. You never fight, and neither of you ever raises his voice. You never get jealous or territorial. Things are going great, right? That's crap. If you want to keep him, you need to be a little less agreeable every now and then.

Preston is a 40-year-old banker from Madison, Wisconsin. He's been living with Paul, 38, for over eight years, and though they have a nice home together, they rarely have sex any more. Preston regularly cruises chat rooms for hookups. Paul knows and says he doesn't really mind. It sounds like a great setup on paper: Paul is not into the sex (or so he says), and Preston gets sex whenever he wants with anyone he wants, as though he were single. Trouble is, Preston is ready to leave because Paul is way too relaxed about their relationship. "If Paul would just get angry about my sleeping with other guys, if he would just tell me I'm not allowed to fuck around, I'd probably not even consider leaving. Fucked up, isn't it? I'd probably be more aggressive about getting Paul into bed with me if he acted up and got mad." Preston is just begging for some boundaries.

For gay men who are accustomed to being sexual outlaws and existing only on the fringe of coupledom, boundaries can be a tough thing. Preston needs to throw a screaming fit one time when Paul comes home too late. "Of course, I'd probably scream right back at first," says Preston, "but at least I'd know that he cares who I fuck, like a husband is supposed to."

Of course, continual hissy fits and ceaseless discussions about ground rules can be grating, so the trick to marking your territory is to do it judiciously. It's cool to get jealous every so often but not regularly. Don't get all *Sleeping With the Enemy* on his ass. Occasional jealousy is a way of setting the limits that you're comfortable with in a relationship. Setting limits is a two-way discussion of course, so when he balks at your trying to run his life ("You're not my keeper, you're being impossible!"), be ready to roll with a few punches. And above all, be ready to compromise. Occasional legitimate jealousy must be curbed before it becomes paranoia, but you're not a fanatic, right? You still have to demonstrate that you care how he behaves in the relationship, or he may misinterpret your confidence as apathy.

NO. 101 Mementos Make the Memories

If you've had a wonderful time with a date or a steady boyfriend at a gallery or the county fair, or if you had a rip-roaring good time in the sack with a one-night stand or a fuck buddy, sending him off with a little memento of your encounter will keep him thinking of you long after the meeting has ended. It's the same theory used for wedding receptions and big parties. The goodies in the gift bag prompt people to remember elements of the party.

A memento? Like what? Say you went to the county fair. Pick up a postcard of that 800-pound fake alligator that you both paid 25 cents to see and mail it to him the next day, with a note saying that you had a good time (if you actually did) and you'd like to see him again. It's easy do the postcard thing if you saw a great gallery show or a museum exhibit together. Postcards are plentiful at galleries and museums, historical sites, and tourist traps. Not only will he remember the great art or the giant margaritas, he'll always associate them with you.

After a rendezvous with a boyfriend in several bathrooms of a crowded mall in Costa Mesa, California, Luke, 23, sent his boyfriend a map brochure of the mall that he got from the information desk. With a red marker, he circled all the bathrooms where they'd fucked. "He was visiting his family out of town, so I mailed it to his parents' house. He called me when he got it, and he laughed for 20 minutes," said Luke. "And now I can't go back to Banana Republic at that mall without popping a boner."

Enjoy Yourself

The ultimate secret to good gay sex is the simplest of all: Enjoy yourself! Here are yet a few more reasons why gay sex is enjoyable.

★ Gay sex is fun!

★ Gay sex is subversive (especially if you're a Republican), so the rebellious among us can enjoy feeling that their predilections, fetishes, kinks, and appetites are forms of protest.

★ Gay sex is natural, as proved by our ever-expanding understanding of psychology and the human sex drive.

★ Gay sex is intimate and passionate, so that the romantics among us can know that the search for a soul mate isn't futile.

★ Gay sex is physical, vital, and even spiritual.

★ Gay sex is a malleable thing: We can shape our sex lives to suit our desires, and we can test our personal boundaries.

★ Good gay sex is a continual learning process. You have to work at it to make your sex life better; that means that you can never get bored, if you use your mind as well as your body. Practice makes perfect, and this practice is fun.

★ Gay sex is anything we want it to be, but if we don't allow ourselves to enjoy our bodies, to revel in our desires, and to explore our passions, then we're missing the point.

★ A healthy sex life and a healthy sexual attitude will improve the overall quality of your life. It's your job to be well-informed about the workings of your body as well as how to keep your sex partners healthy and satisfied, how to explore your sexuality, and how to banish your feelings of shame and embarrassment. Relish your life—that's why you're here!